**THE LONG-LOST AUTOBIOGRAPHY OF
GEORGES MÉLIÈS, FATHER OF SCI-FI
AND FANTASY CINEMA**
by GEORGES MÉLIÈS and JON SPIRA

ISBN (hardback): 978-0-9957356-44
ISBN (e-book): 978-0-9957356-51

First published 2019 by Jon Spira
Copyright © Jon Spira

Print Edition
First edition May 2019

The right of Jon Spira to be identified as the author of this work (with the exception of the included texts previously published as *Mes Memoires* and *Cinematic Views* both by George Méliès) has been asserted by him in accordance with the Copyright, Designs and Patents Act 1988.

The right of Jon Spira to be identified as the copyright-holder of this English translation of *Mes Memoires* and *Cinematic Views* by George Méliès has been asserted by him in accordance with the Copyright, Designs and Patents Act 1988.

All rights reserved, No part of this publication may be reproduced, stored in or introduced into a retrieval system, or transmitted, in any form, or by any means (electronic, mechanical, photocopying, recording or otherwise) without the prior written permission of the publisher. Any person who does any unauthorized act in relation to this publication may be liable to criminal prosecution and civil claims for damages.

A CIP catalogue record for this book is available from the British Library.

This book is sold subject to the condition that it shall not, by way of trade or otherwise, be lent, re-sold, hired out, or otherwise circulated without the publisher's prior consent in any form of binding or cover other than that which it is published and without a similar condition including this condition being imposed upon the subsequent purchaser.

THE LONG-LOST AUTOBIOGRAPHY OF GEORGES MÉLIÈS, FATHER OF SCI-FI AND FANTASY CINEMA

by

GEORGES MÉLIÈS

With annotation and
supporting material by
JON SPIRA

English translation by IAN NIXON

Illustrated by LUCY COLLIN

Design and layout by SIMON MINTER

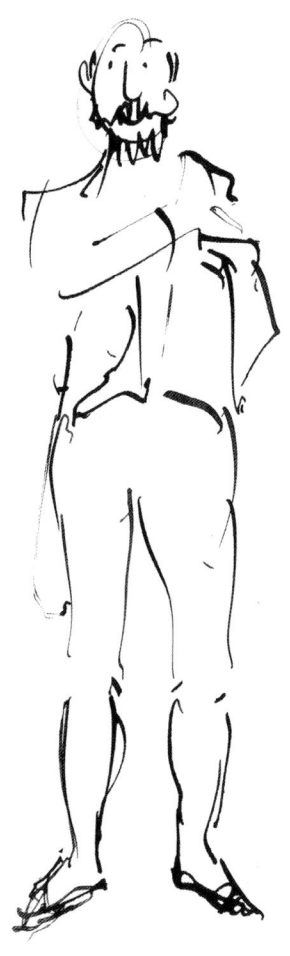

Portrait of George Méliès by Graham Humphreys

CONTENTS

Angels 6

Introduction
Méliès and Me 11
Hopes, Tropes and Scopes 19

Life and Work
An Introduction to the Following Text 35
The Life and Work of One of the World's Earliest Pioneers of Cinema,
Georges Méliès, Creator of Film as Spectacle 38
Translation of *Cinematic Views* 137
The Other Méliès 157
George Méliès Filmography 163

Interviews
Interview with Serge Bromberg 184
Interview with Bryony Dixon 194
Interview with Michel Gondry 200

In Closing
Thanks 202
Select Bibliography 205
About the Authors 208

ANGELS

THIS PROJECT WAS MADE POSSIBLE THROUGH THE PATRONAGE OF THESE ANGELS…

A.J. Mell
Abhilash Sarhadi
Adam Savje
Alan Hardy
Alan Stephen
Alessa0
Alexander von Schlinke
Ali Catterall
Alison McMahan
Alma Headland
Andrew Fisher
Andrew Kelly
Andrew Kenny
Andy Hollingworth
Andy Ross
Andy Veness
Arron Capone-Langan
Astrô Rondon
Becky Lorberfeld
Ben Lavington Martin
Bernd Herzogenrath
Beth Accomando
Beth Ann Gallagher
Boaz Halachmi
Brian R. Boisvert
Brian Robinson
Brian Serpa
Cameo Wood
Cameron Orme
Cato Vandrare
Chad Tremblay
Charles Burkart
Charles D. Moisant
Charles de Lauzirika
Chris Edwards
Chris L White
Chris Mitchell
Christian A. Zschammer
Christian Engblom
Christian Monggaard
Christian Schellenberger
Christian Undeutsch
Christian Walther
Christina Petersen
Christopher Strange
Claire Vaughan
Cleo Hanaway-Oakley
Colin Dickey
Collector's Shangri-La
Constantine Nasr
Craig Tonks
Dale C. Barker
Dana Snyder
Daniel Cook
Dave Roberts
David
David A Brown
David Barraclough
David Lee Brown
David Chamberlain
David Cotelessa
David Elvis Leeming
David Hasler
David Lockwood
David Stewart
Davide Giurlando
Deadly
Didier Gertsch
DKE Toys
Dom Del Gaudio
Dominic Halford
Donna Hill
Doug Thornton
Eisenhower PLD
Elias Savada
Ellen Jane Keenan
Elliot Sutherland
Elsa Cerqueira
Emil Lønberg Lolk
Enrique Dueñas
Eon Davidson
Eric Mattlin
Erick Larson
Farah Ismail
Florian Schiffmann
Franck Gurrieri
Frank Visintini
Gary Lawrence
Gary Marsh
Genevieve RM Fecteau
Georgia Young
Giles Edwards
Godfrey DiGiorgi
Graham Humphreys
Greg Bachar
Guy Ratki
Hank Starrs
Hansen Li
Helder Guimarães
Henrik Sanderbo
Iain M Rowbottom
Iain Potter
Ian Hopkins
Is Amavizca
Jacob W. Fleming
James R. Wenle

Angels

James Hickman	Laurens Wilming	Natalia & Gust	Seanetta Allsass
James von Boeckmann	Laurie Munro Gordon	Nicolas Pierron	Shane O'Reilly
Jae Cope	Lawrence Sutcliffe	Nicholas Freeston	Shannon Marrs
Javier Torres	Lee Wrona	Nick Deakin	Shelley Cao
Jean-Michel Decombe	Lester Frank Callif	Patricia Suchy	Shoubna Naika-Taylor
Jeff B.	LF	Patrick Harley	Sigurður Páll Guðbjartsson
Jennifer Anne Benton	Linda Wenzelburger	Patrick J Vaz	Simon Atkin
Jennifer Keenan	Liz Torokfalvy	Patrick May	Simon Field
Jerry Mosher	Luis Vázquez	Patrick Migneault	Simon Trigwell
Jesús Bravo	Maccewill J D Yip	Patrick/Jacqui Reimann	Simone Savogin
Jo Anseeuw	Malcolm Cleugh	Paul Arpaia	Simon Tainton
Joel Fenster	Marcio Hashimoto	Peggy Kimbell	Spencer Sundell
John Davenport	Marek Čermák	Peter Hanink	Stefania Forlini
John Landis	Mariah Leah Jensen	Peter Nagy	Stephan Friedt
John Stewart Muller	Mark Giltrow	Phil Clements	Stephen Duignan
Joleigh Doner	Mark Rogerson	Phill Warren	Steven Tsai
Jonathan Cohn	Marshall-Breton	R Paul Wilson	Steven Wellerling
Jonathan Marlow	Martin Kudlac	Rahul Venugopal	Stuart Barr
Jonathan R Freed	Matt Hilton	Rainer Clodius	Susanne Abetti
Jonathan J Walker	Matt Large	Ramarren	Suzanne Melton
Jörg Müller-Kindt	Matthew McCroskey	Randy Brill	Talal Alyouha
Jörg Tragert	Matthew Stanosz	Ricardo Barrig	Tara Bayes
Joseph Forrer	Max Krause	Rich House	Taylor White
Josh	Maximilian Robert Lockwood	Richard Kaufman	Thomas Amborn
Julian Harding	Michael Skazick	Richard Maher	Thomas Fayne
Julian Kemp	Michael Aus	Rick Daub	Thomas Negovan
Karlina Harlow Dawn	Michael B. Johnson	Robert Byrne	Tim Elwell
Karma Christine Salvato	Michael Canepa	Robert Hsu	Tim O'Brien
Keith Kasper	Michael Feldman	Robert Riley-Mercado	Tim Rosenberger
Kevin Goodman	Michael Marlatt	Robert Wells	Tom Buckley
Kevin James	Michael Peterson	Robin	Topher Davila
Kevin Niezurawski	Miguel Rodriguez	Robindra Neogi	Toronto Silent Film Festival
Kevin O'Brien	Mike DeLisa	Roger Strahl	Traci & Brian Belanger
Khui Wong	Mike Elizalde	Ronnie Elliott	Ulrich Ruedel
Kirk Larson	Mike L'Alouette	Rosalie Greener	Victoria Langford
Kit M	Mike McFarland	Sandra DeKay	Vijay Varman
Kristin Selzer	Mike Meltzer	Sarah Paling	Vincent Liu
Kyle Honzik	MoonTech Studios	Scott Bishop	Vitas Varnas
Lachlan Hazelton	Mudd Law	Scott Galey	Wren Godwin
Lance Bohy	Nancy Fornoville	Dr Scott Wilson	Yann Sicamois

THIS BOOK IS DEDICATED TO RENEE JEANNE

INTRODUCTION

Méliès and Me

Jon Spira

I love autobiographies. I also love film. So, it stands to reason that film autobiographies are very, very much my thing.

The truth is, I don't read much else. I might read one fiction book per year, mainly to get some variety in my literary diet, and almost without fail each year I read the last page of that fiction book and close it with a thankful sigh. Truth is stranger than fiction and autobiography is stranger than truth. More often than not, an autobiography is the only book the author will ever write and that, in itself, this raw perspective on what they consider is worth talking about and what is not, often gives a greater insight into the mind of the person than their words. Darth Vader actor Dave Prowse, for example, devotes an entire chapter (Chapter 8: Windows of Opportunity) of his autobiography (*Straight From The Force's Mouth: The Autobiography of Dave Prowse MBE*) to naming and shaming a company who did a bad job replacing the windows in his house.

I should say at this point, that I'm using 'autobiography' as a catch-all term for autobiography (a self-penned life chronology), memoir (a self-penned recollection of a certain moment in the author's life) and, sometimes, biography (a chronology of a life written by someone else). I'm far less fond of biography because, again, between the lines we often find out as much about the author as the subject. I'm aware of the irony of writing that, in the introduction of what is essentially a mash-up of autobiography and biography.

The first autobiography I ever read, technically a memoir, was *The Close Encounters of the Third Kind diary* by Bob Balaban, which remains by far the best book I've ever read on the experience of making films. Buying it as a precocious 12 year old, I expected a blow-by-blow account of how Spielberg achieved his masterpiece but was confused and delighted to find a story largely concerned with the neuroses of a character actor who has lied about his ability to speak French and consequently finds himself charged with looking after Francois Truffaut who spoke little English. It was concerned less with the facts of a life in film as the feelings. The insecurities, petty squabbles and petty victories. The moments of levity and gloom. The fascinating bridge between real life and the fantasy of Hollywood.

From that point on, for the next thirty years, my appetite was insatiable. I immediately followed that book with *Wired* – Bob Woodward's harrowing account of John Belushi's last days. I had been expecting something a little more fun. But it was exactly that thwarted expectation which has led me to be very egalitarian in my reading. I will happily read the autobiography of absolutely anybody associated with the world of film. I've devoured the wry and macho tales of stuntmen Hal Needham and Vic Armstrong. The canny and sharp observations of screenwriters David Mamet and William Goldman. The bizarre ascendancy to and appropriation of power stories of 70s/80s studio heads Robert Evans and Dawn Steel especially when compared to the bullish warmth of Jack Warner's *My First Hundred Years in Hollywood*. The delightful bitchiness of producer Julia Phillips's books and I should mention the Don Simpson biography *High Concept* here as it is one of the most notable books about the life of a Hollywood producer but it is such a harrowing and disgusting story I gave my copy to a charity shop the day I finished it, I didn't want it in the house. There is no shortage of film director autobiographies. Although challenging the form, Hitchcock/Truffaut has never been bettered. For a while, Faber and Faber published their 'on' series in which directors were invited to give a chronological oral history of themselves and their work – *Scorsese on Scorsese, Schrader on Schrader, Altman on Altman, Woody Allen on Woody Allen, Tim Burton on Tim Burton*. I don't know why they stopped. Of course, the majority of film autobiographies are from the stars and they vary wildly in outlook and self-regard. From the breathless impishness of Errol Flynn's posthumously published *My Wicked, Wicked Ways*, a truly hilarious account of a life lived reckless (which often leaves the reader slack-jawed and agog; he spends a whole page detailing how he created a living 'human centipede' with a flock of ducks, some bacon and a ball of string) to the literary eloquence of Charlie Chaplin's reflection of a life with one foot in abject poverty and the other in gaudy wealth.

My favourite bizarre autobiography is Sean Astin's exhausting, yet addicting, *There and Back Again: An Actor's Tale* which is perhaps the finest example of an author writing entirely between the lines. It has a tarnished, peeling, thin, yet persistent veneer of magnanimity which spectacularly fails to hide the bitterness and passive-aggression he seems to feel for everybody he has ever met.

My overall favourite autobiography is *Herself* by Elsa Lanchester. A witty, affectionate, sly and barbed take on her life from the Suffragette marches to the Bloomsbury literary elite to the golden age of Hollywood. The narrative spine of the book is her four-decade marriage to Charles Laughton, who was actively, although not openly, gay. A high point in the book is the moment he confesses to her in light of an encounter he had in her absence and her measured response "Fine, okay, but get rid of the sofa."

There are a lot of books out there which will purport to tell you the whole history of film but in some ways my life-long project has been to learn that story not from academics but from the testimonies of those who built it.

Last year, I finally got around to reading *Harpo Speaks*, the extremely weighty tome of autobiography from Harpo Marx. For a long time, I had been put off not just by the size and, frankly, price of it but also the suspicion that it will tell the exact same story as his brother's excellent book *Groucho & Me*. I couldn't have been more wrong; perhaps because he knew Groucho had already covered their career, this is a personal telling of a life from the streets to the elites. The book is almost entirely concerned with his life away from performance – his family and his friends. His times as a part of Dorothy Parker's circle and William Randolph Hearst's castle guest. Then his gentle segue into the life of a father in his later years. It's a humble, human book about public persona and private reality.

It was with sadness that I put that book down for the last time and realised I didn't have another in waiting. Who did I want to know about? I had recently read the Faber and

Faber book of letters written by the Lumiere Brothers and was keen to revisit that period. Méliès. Of course, Méliès. How had I never read his autobiography? I guess I'd never happened upon it.

I don't remember when I was first aware of Méliès, it feels like he's always been there, somewhere. I can imagine, like all Western male film buffs of my generation, he was a footnote in a book about *Star Wars*. Maybe my film buff dad had shown me a picture in one of his books as he saw my burgeoning affection for sci-fi. And we all know which picture.

The one, simple, baseline thing that everyone who knows about film knows about Georges Méliès is that he is the man who put the rocket in the eye of the moon. And that is where, I suspect, most people's knowledge of him begins and ends. It's where mine did for a long time. As a teenager, before the advent of YouTube or boutique DVD labels, there simply wasn't a lot of Méliès out there. *A Trip to the Moon* was really the only work available in any accessible form, most of his work was believed long-gone. But I read about him and fostered a love and respect for him. When I got into the band The Wonder Stuff at the age of 15, I was delighted to see that they had selected Méliès's moon as the cover art for their album *HUP*. I had no idea why. I still have no idea why but I know when my t-shirt bearing this image and their logo fell to pieces, I immediately replaced it.

I picked up bits of information on Méliès as I grew older and when Flicker Alley released their stunning DVD box set in 2008, I finally got to properly engage with his astounding body of work. Five years later, entirely by chance on a trip to Barcelona, I discovered a huge exhibition of the Cinematheque Francais archive of what remains of his life and work. I spent hours surrounded by his original paintings, notes, documents, costumes, props, posters and equipment and marveled at how much of it survived since, for so long, we had assumed so few of his films had. I have had the poster from that exhibition on my living room wall ever since. And there have been four different living rooms in that time. I really don't know why it took me so long to get around to hunting out his autobiography, but now was the moment.

I knew that one existed as some years ago I'd seen a photo of Charlie Chaplin taking a break on the set of Monsieur Verdoux, reading a book which simply bore what looked like Méliès's signature on the cover.

My first stop was Amazon UK and here's what I found, in order: a critical appreciation of *A Trip To The Moon*; a very small Italian language book simply called *Georges Méliès* with no description of contents; Elizabeth Ezra's lively but heavily academic and analytical book from Manchester University Press; a catalogue from a 1993 exhibition at London's much-missed Museum of the Moving Image. And then just a deluge of mainly academic, largely foreign-language and almost entirely out-of-print books. On the third page, I spotted a biography written by his great-granddaughter but, upon researching, I discovered that this had never been translated into English. The closest thing that I eventually found, upon heavier research, was Paul Hammond's *Marvellous Méliès*, which is a lovely read but has been out of print for 44 years.

My take-away from this hunt was that there was not only no Méliès autobiography, there was no – in the traditional sense – biography of him. An accessible, chronological, biographical summation of his life and work which was in English and in print.

In the search, I had not found the book that Chaplin was reading in that photo. So, assuming it must have been written in French, I armed myself with Google Translate and a free afternoon and started to scour French book websites to see what I could find.

I quickly found out that this book was not his autobiography but a posthumously released biography of him by respected French film historian Maurice Bessy and co-founder of *Cahiers du Cinema*, Joseph Lo Duca. Research told me that this was published only once – in 1945 – as a limited edition by a publisher called Prisma Editions. I just wanted a copy. I knew it would probably result in many hours hunched over Google Translate but I wanted a copy of the book Chaplin seemed to be enjoying.

It took a lot of time on eBay, Abe Books and various websites to find a copy in decent condition and my price range but eventually I succeeded. When it arrived, it was a thing of beauty but also an object of mystery. The title page read:

MAURICE BESSY et LO DUCA
GEORGES MÉLIÈS
MAGE
et
"MES MÉMOIRES"
par
MÉLIÈS

So, slightly confusingly, it appeared it was a biography of the man but also an autobiography. Which is what it was. After the book and after the bibliography and after a section called 'All That Remains', which is a collection of images from the missing films, you get a printed transcription of Méliès's memoirs.

This was, by far, the best part of the book and I thought it weird and sad that it was merely an added bonus.

Flicking through the book subsequently, I noticed a leaf at the front which I had previously ignored, taking it to be some kind of copyright notice. It wasn't. It translated roughly as:

"There are 2,000 copies of this book, including 1,500 numbered from 501 to 2,000 constituting the original edition and 500 copies numbered from 1 to 500, accompanied by a facsimile reproduction of the manuscript 'Mes Memoires' by Georges Méliès."

So began my journey to track down a copy from the first 500 which included the facsimile.

These are hard to find. Initial research told me that the first 500 appeared to have a black cover rather than red, but in some photos it looked a bit green. I couldn't tell if this was due to poor lighting or perhaps the books themselves fading. Copies like this cropped up but none of them had the manuscript, so I held tight. It turned out that the green covered editions were their own thing, but I'll get onto that…

Eventually, I found a black copy online, offered by a bookseller in rural France. He was impressively poor at communicating and, although I could see the first, and potentially, last page of the facsimile, I was still unsure whether I'd be getting the whole thing and whether it was even in Méliès's own handwriting – but I put a chunk of money down, rolled the dice and waited.

It arrived in good condition. The numbering was in line with the edition – I had copy no. 321 and tucked away in a little pouch at the back was not only the full facsimile but also a facsimile business card.

Seeing how beautiful the facsimile was, how exciting it was to see Méliès's own handwriting, corrections, notes and annotations, also filled me with outrage that this had languished so long in obscurity. I knew there were a lot of people like me who would want their own copy. And that was when I decided to launch the Kickstarter campaign which funded the publication of this book.

The campaign itself was a wild ride, this was my fifth successful crowdfunding project and the most backed of them all. This lead to unexpected attention from the media and other corners, including the delight of garnering the support of some of my favourite filmmakers including John Landis and Joe Dante. A begrudging acceptance of the recognised definition of the term 'long-lost' opened up a conversation between myself and Méliès's great-granddaughter Anne-Marie.

She gave me some interesting background on the book; To begin with, she is not a fan of *Mage* and the route to which the manuscript became included was not a straightforward one. Being a part of the book, I had assumed that Méliès had sent the original manuscript to the two authors as a factual basis and they had decided to include it complete as an added feature. This appears to not have been the case. As Anne-Marie describes it, from the files and contracts of her association:

"In 1933, a French journalist asked Méliès to write his Memoirs. Then this text was sent to Italy in 1936, because the League of Nations had instructed Italy to publish a Dictionary of Illustrious Men. Italy was excluded from the League of Nations after it had invaded Ethiopia. This manuscript was however published by the Italian magazine *Cinema* in 1938. Then in 1940, this magazine sold the manuscript of the Memoirs to Mr. Lo Duca, who became the owner of the papers (but not of the copyrights). May be a trouble story…"

She also told me that she felt that *Mage* was full of factual errors and had been denounced as such upon release. She confirms that Prisma were licensed to produce 2,000 copies and that the first 500 of these were indeed the black edition with the facsimile and that she also holds a copy of the red edition which did not come with the facsimile. But then she told me about the green edition.

She refers to this as the "wild" edition. It seems that Prisma released these secretly, without informing the Méliès family, to avoid paying them for the copyrights on the text or illustrations. She claims there are two "wild" editions, both with green covers. One green edition came with the facsimile, one without. Neither she, nor I, have seen a green edition numbered above 3,000 (the green edition has the same text at the front of the book, claiming only 2,000 copies exist, yet they are numbered above 2,000), so it seems safe to assume that there were 1,000 of the green edition. However, I've looked into this a lot online and can't find any evidence of a wild edition with the facsimile. Which is not to say they didn't exist but examples of all other three editions (black, red, green without facsimile) are all, if not available to buy, available to see pictures of online. A wild edition with facsimile is not something that there appears to be evidence of.

She also told me that in 1961, a company called Editions JJ Pauvert released a paperback reissue of the book to celebrate the Méliès centenary. This also did not come with a facsimile. They publicly claimed also to only be releasing 2,000 copies but their contract with the Méliès family allowed for 5,000.

When I had embarked upon the campaign, it had been my understanding that:

1. This book had been out of print since 1945
2. Only 2,000 copies of the Bessy/Lo Duca book existed
3. Only 500 copies of the manuscript facsimile were ever released.

Anne-Marie's information changed that to:

1. This book has been out of print since 1961
2. It seems that 3,000 copies of the Bessy/Lo Duca book existed
3. There is a possibility that 1,000 copies of the manuscript facsimile were released.

What had not changed, however, was my fervent belief that this incredibly important testimony as to the life of the man who had brought magic to cinema was an obscure, hard-to-find document which deserved to be known and available to all who love film. And that is why you are holding this book in your hands.

Like all the best autobiographies, the character of the author transcends the work. It was written in 1937, the year before he died. Méliès was 77 years old and very well aware of his hallowed place in film history. Tetchily aware. This is a man who does not want to be remembered merely for his fantasies: he was a man of greater achievement than that and lobbies to be acknowledged accordingly. We find a man not humbled by poverty but still angry at those he perceived to have landed him there. Yet this is not a diatribe, this is an emotionally honest reflection and summation of his life. Méliès writes in the third person. I'm not sure why. For the briefest, stupidest, moment, I considered changing it to first person for this book but quickly realised that perhaps the very fact he made this choice tells us something further about his character.

Bringing Méliès's autobiography into the light, commissioning its translation, producing the supporting material and making it accessible and available to the film-loving community has been a fantastic experience. I hope you enjoy it. ★

Jon Spira
London, 2019

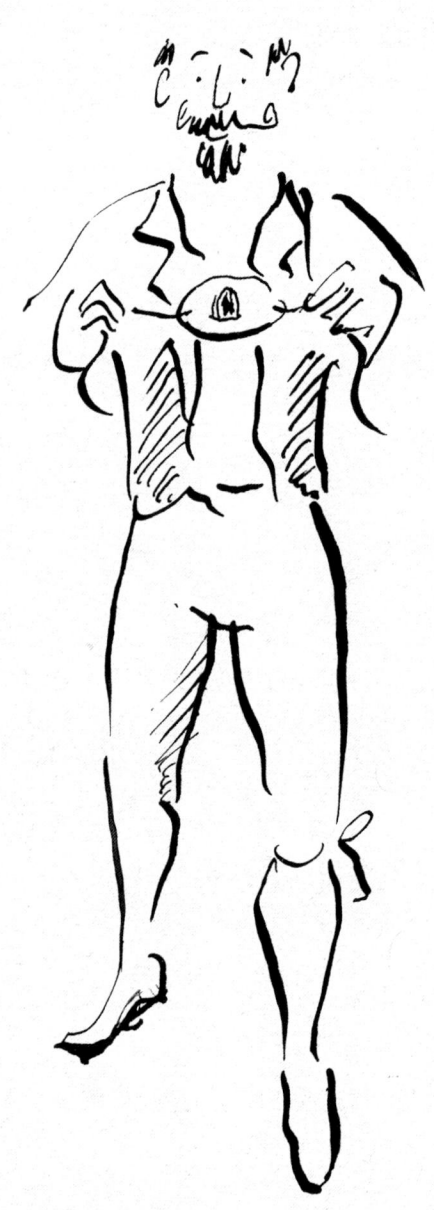

Hopes, Tropes and Scopes

The Moving Image Before Méliès

On 28th December 1895, in the Salon Indien room in the basement of the Grand Cafe in Paris, film history, as we know it, began. Georges Méliès joined a small audience in observing the two brilliant sons of his friend Charles-Antoine Lumiere unveil their creation for the first time in public. Using their patented Cinematographe machine, they projected moving photographic images through the darkness onto a screen.

This moment is widely accepted as the birth of film. It was certainly the eureka moment which led Méliès to go on to perhaps lay the creative foundations of what we now recognise to be narrative cinema. The importance of what happened in that room is undeniable. I'd like to spirit you forward 25 years, before dragging you back significantly more, to another room, of far less importance.

In the Connaught Rooms, a grand meeting space in London, England, on the 5th of May 1921, Lord Beaverbrook chaired a meeting of representatives of the British film industry. Cinema, not three decades old, was big business and that business was in disarray. Between the film producers and the film exhibitors stood the renters – the middle-men – who dictated the terms: which cinemas could have which films for how long and what level of exclusivity for what fees and what percentage of the door. With the vast percentage of these films being American in origin, it seemed like both the British producers and British exhibitors were in need of some form of help. The meeting was always going to have a charged atmosphere. So much money, so many businesses and personal finances depended upon the outcome.

Film has always sat somewhere on the outside edge of what we perceive to be culture. Perhaps it is seen to lack the refinement of theatre, the purity of art, the intelligence of literature and the direct authenticity of music. Film was the first artform born into the capitalist world and has never fully shaken off that vulgarity of association. It has always required an investment to produce and a purchase to consume. In the Connaught Rooms that day, it is unlikely that anybody was discussing the creative merits of the medium.

In amongst the pack of angry businessmen, a stranger – an impoverished old man in a shabby suit – cleared his throat. Using what little energy he had, he took to his feet and passionately advocated for a fair solution to be found. His voice was weak and Beaverbrook urged him to make his way to the platform to be better heard. Having said his piece, the man made his way back to his seat and died.

This man, William Friese-Greene, had already been a ghost when he entered that room. He had belonged to the brief period in time when film was not a commodity but a delightful pursuit. A moment in which some of the sharpest and most imaginative minds of the age challenged themselves to create a method of capturing and displaying photographic images which moved.

Many players contributed, purposefully and unwittingly, to the point at which Georges Méliès was able to capture and then project his first film. The inception of cinema is a messy confluence of theory, machinery, experimentation, performance, happy accident and bitter failure. With hindsight, the event of cinema seems almost inevitable in the endlessly innovative 1890s where many enlightened minds were quite separately dabbling in the same areas of research. I'd like to map a path for you, through this landscape of largely-forgotten giants upon whose shoulders Méliès had to stand to become the icon that he is today.

There is no shortage of moments that one could choose to herald as the moment that cinema began. Some documented, many not. Human beings have always been enchanted by flickering light in the darkness; the magic lantern shows (of which Méliès's were recognised as some of the best in the world) were perhaps the first time that humans gathered in a darkened room to watch projected light tell stories. Unless you count the shadow puppets which were already enchanting Indonesian audiences some three thousand years previously. Or hand shadows on cave walls from the light of the earliest fires. These are all entertainments provided by projected light in a darkened space, which is certainly the bedrock science of cinema, but what were the occurrences which led humanity towards the unified goal of projecting light through a moving strip of sequential, individual, photographic images to capture and replay life as a moving image?

To my mind, our story actually begins with a carriage wheel. Or, perhaps I should say, it commences, initiates, starts, opens, activates or originates with a carriage wheel. Specifically, a carriage wheel as seen by one Peter Mark Roget. Roget was primarily a physician although he was also a lexicographer and theologian. Popular history remembers him now almost exclusively as the creator of the Thesaurus to which he gave his name but Roget's was a curiosity unbound.

Amongst the many papers he wrote (the most intriguingly titled undoubtedly being *Animal and Vegetable Physiology considered with reference to Natural Theology* (1834)) was one presented on the 9th December 1824 entitled *Explanation Of An Optical Deception In The Appearance Of The Spokes Of*

a Wheel When Seen Through Vertical Apertures, which contains the equation which set film in motion. By observing the illusion of the curvature of wheel spokes whilst passing a palisade or a Venetian window blind, Roget contended that the human retina was able to temporarily retain an image of something after that thing had been removed. Roget was wrong, motion perception is to do with the brain rather than the eye, but he had neatly established (fixed, rooted, secured...) the notion that a strobing effect created a rather nifty optical illusion.

In the months following Roget's paper, another British physician John Ayrton Paris, better known for the discovery that exposure to arsenic fumes could lead to scrotal skin cancer, 'invented' the Thaumatrope. The Thaumatrope, a perennial children's toy, is a disc suspended on two strings, printed on both sides with different images which, when wound tight and allowed to spin at a high speed, combines them. The most famous example bears a bird on one side and a cage on the other, leading to an image of a caged bird. I used the word invented in inverted commas because this principle had been around for a long time before being formalised. In fact, the man credited as the "father of the computer", mathematician Charles Babbage, later laid claim to having invented the very same object with geologist William Henry Fitton some years earlier, as a lark which they failed to pursue after producing the first few prototypes. There have since been discovered crude prehistoric examples of this very same principle but Paris was the man who brought it to the world in this pregnant moment.

Roget's paper also inspired the Belgian physicist Joseph Plateau. Plateau, whose main area of interest was actually soap bubbles, was so fascinated by the science of the persistence of luminous impression on the retina that he once conducted an experiment which involved him staring into the sun for 25 minutes. He died blind. At some point between these two events, however, Plateau produced a practical extraction of Roget's basic concept.

He had been toying with movement-related optical illusions even before reading Roget's paper. As a student, he had noticed that when he looked through two fast-spinning concentric cog-wheels moving in different directions, he was presented with the image of a still cog. From this, Plateau created the Anorthoscope. A fascinating, contraption featuring an anamorphic – highly stretched circular – image painted onto a disc. When this disc is spun at a high speed and viewed through a black disc with four slits cut into it, which is spinning at a high speed in the opposite direction, the anamorphic image looks stationary and normal.

Plateau was friendly with Michael Faraday (of Faraday's Cage fame) who had also been intrigued by this area of study. It was Faraday who had advised Plateau to incorporate a mirror into the equation and this led to Plateau's greatest contribution to the field of the moving image.

The Phenakistoscope was a free-spinning circular piece of cardboard mounted in the middle to a wooden handle. Along the outside edge were a series of cut-out slits. On the body of the circle was a ring of images that we would now recognise as the basis of animation – each image conveying one frame of movement advanced from the previous. If you stood facing a mirror, held the device in front of you and gave it a spin, looking through the strobing slits at the mirror you would see the animation at a fixed point. The faster you spun, the faster it moved. If there was an equal number of slits, the moving image remained in a fixed position; if there were fewer, it would move around the wheel whilst animating. This became a hit when produced commercially but essentially the technology went no further than novelty at this moment.

Whilst Plateau was inventing the Phenakistoscope, Simon Von Stampfer, a mathematician in Vienna, had the same idea. Also inspired by Faraday's work, he conceived essentially the same device but named it the Stroboscope. In July 1833, Stampfer published a pamphlet detailing his workin which he suggested that the concept need not only be applied to a cardboard disc. The concept could also be applied to a cylinder or a looped strip of paper or canvas stretched around two parallel rollers – somewhat like the mechanism for a projector, minus the light bulb.

Stampfer's suggestions remained just that, with no practical demonstrations produced, but he was on to something. The cylinder would form the next evolution of the moving image.

A year later, in 1834, British mathematician William George Horner, acknowledging the work of Plateau, Faraday and Roget, claimed to have created a device which simplified the process of animating a still image and removed the requirement of a mirror. His Dædalum was a spinning drum with the images printed on the inside edge and the slits between them. When it was spun, any number of people standing around it could watch the animation at the same time.

The Dædalum is now better known as the Zoetrope.

The Zoetrope kicked around as a novelty, not finding widespread commercial success until the 1860s, at which point it became a beloved staple of the toy chest. With the addition of changeable paper loops to place inside the drum, the Zoetrope became perhaps the most enduring of all pre-cinema novelties.

At this point you might be wondering, as I was, why all of these elaborately-named inventions ended in either a 'scope' or a 'trope'. I asked lexicographer Susie Dent if she could explain this to me. She replied that "One is all about movement, the other about seeing". A 'trope' is a device which actively demonstrates movement, a 'scope' is a device which allows the eye to

see movement. But not every development in this timeline is a scope or trope.

It's almost surprising to realise that the most simple and widespread animation device surfaced quite a while *after* these machines. It was not until 1868 that the world first saw the flip book (or flick book). The idea first appears in a patent from one John Barnes Linnett, a lithographic printer from Birmingham in England and is registered as the Kineograph.

The flip book is, of course, simplicity itself and it's a wonder that this didn't precede the spinning wheel concepts. A book, with a different sequential image on each page which, when a thumb is run along the corner, produces the illusion of motion.

The flip book is the moment that the moving image moves from optical illusion novelty to storytelling for the one simple reason that it takes the seismic jump from a circular sequence to a linear narrative. Gone was the infinite repetition of a fixed number of frames and slits. The only thing limiting the length of the story told now was the size of the viewer's hands.

All of this experimentation around the concept of the moving image was just that. In some ways it could be viewed as the folly of brilliant minds. All of the key developers of these concepts and machines are far better known for their work in other areas and whenever their findings in this field were published they seemed to be appropriated into the manufacture of mere novelties. None of this is cinema as we know it. But it has fertilized the soil. And in 1872, the first steps towards the mechanised illuminated projection of sequential photographic images were unwittingly taken. All of these men, their ideas and their contraptions undoubtedly contributed to the moment of conception, but personally, I like to think that cinema as we know it came about because of an argument.

In 1872, former Governor of California Leland Stanford – you might know his name from the university he founded – had many interests: a couple of vineyards, a part-ownership in Wells Fargo, a life insurance company (still running today as Pacific Life) and, as a hobby, a thoroughbred horse farm in Palo Alto. It was here that, apparently untroubled by loftier concerns, Leland and his pals debated furiously the ultimate question: When a horse ran, did all four of its hooves leave the ground or was one always still in contact with it? We can only imagine how, in those pre-internet days, free from distraction, they must have argued their cases back and forth and, without assistance from Yahoo Answers or Snopes, how vexed they must have become in not actually knowing either way.

Stanford, ever the pragmatist, contracted exotically-named photographer Eadweard Muybridge (born Edward Muggeridge in Kingston-upon-Thames, England) to find a way to settle the debate. Over the next few years, Muybridge set up shop in Stanford's horse farm (now the campus of Stanford University) to achieve this. Using a row of 12 equally-distanced cameras and triggers, a horse was ridden past them and the first 'moving' photographic image was born. Film got its first starlet when the study was released titled *Sallie Gardner at a Gallop*, better known now as *The Horse in Motion*.

Some time later, Muybridge copied these photos into silhouette paintings on a glass disc and loaded them into his invention, the Zoopraxiscope. Combining the spinning wheel of the zoetrope with the projected light of the magic lantern, Muybridge's lectures, with little fanfare, featured the first instances of projected natural movement. When this led, in 1893 to a Zoopraxagraphical Hall being built at the Chicago World Fair in which Muybridge delivered his lectures to a paying public audience, he unwittingly created the world's first commercial cinema.

Muybridge dedicated the rest of his career to the study of anatomical motion through photography. Although he also found time to murder his wife's lover and get acquitted on the grounds of justifiable homicide (Philip Glass wrote a libretto about this incident). In his time working at the University of Pennsylvania he captured over 100,000 photographic images of animal and human locomotion.

In the interest of documenting human locomotion, Muybridge, like so many artists, entered his 'nude' period. Along with the standard and academically important studies of naked people walking, running, jumping and ascending and descending stairs, Muybridge also treats us to some unexpected deviations into naked bricklaying, horse-shoeing, garden roller dragging, child spanking, kicking a hat and the coquettishly naughty 'stooping, and rolling a stone on the ground'. All of this formed constituent parts of his career-defining portfolio *Animal Locomotion: an Electro-Photographic Investigation of Connective Phases of Animal Movements*. It also arguably provided the raw components for the origin of the 'blue' movie.

With Muybridge more concerned with academia and cinema's first star Ms Gardner long-since consigned to the glue factory, it was for someone else to build on this achievement. That someone met with Muybridge on the 27th February 1888 and, within a year, would bring the illuminated (if not yet projected) moving photographic image to the masses.

That someone would also become a very familiar name to Méliès, spoken by him in anger more often than respect: Thomas Edison.

It would be hard to think of anybody who could be so comprehensively credited with bringing humanity into modernity more than Mr Edison. Regarded as the inventor of electric light and the lightbulb, with his phonoscope he made possible for the first time sound recording and playback. He is also credited with creating motion pictures and digital electronic communications. By the end of his sixty-two years of work, he held over a thousand separate patents. He wasn't just an outstanding scientist, he was an outstanding businessman and an epoch-making entrepreneur. Sadly, his brilliance was somewhat matched by his reputation for ethically questionable practices.

Edison's Research & Development Laboratory in Mineo Park, New Jersey, was the first of its type, a huge, sprawling facility in which all of his ideas and whims were dragged into being by a team of some of the finest scientific and mathematical minds of the generation. Once these ideas were operational, Edison also had the infrastructure for the global commercial exploitation of them. So, whilst in many cases Edison came up with an idea for a technology he would like to see, it was often the people who worked for him, and it would seem some who did not, who made the actual discoveries and breakthroughs which Edison patented and claimed his own.

Based, one could assume, on Muybridge's work, Edison tasked a Scotsman in his employ – William Dickson – with creating a machine which could do for the eye what his Phonograph could do for the ear. At this point, to capture 24 frames of motion, a device would require 24 lenses. The quest for the single lens motion picture camera had begun. Several people were working towards this end, and not just in Edison's employ, and all were aware that it would require a narrow strip of film or paper which could be pulled precisely through the camera mechanically with each frame being exposed separately.

During the development of what would be known as the Kinetoscope, Dickson shot what has been referred to as the first ever motion picture captured on photographic film – *Monkeyshines no 1*. Just a few seconds long and of a blurry person in white standing still but moving their arms about, it's not apparent what they are doing. The footage, which survives today, is out of focus and ethereal. Creepy, even. Perhaps the film wasn't held stable enough for the lens to focus.

The key to successfully pioneering a solution to record and project film cleanly was perforation - the little holes at the side of a strip of film which allow the strip to be carried past the lens and shutter system with precision.

This is not to say that others hadn't already managed to drag a piece of film past a lens mechanically. In 1889, Edison had visited Étienne-Jules Marey in France. Marey was already working with flexible film strips in his chronophotographic gun invention, which could be considered the world's first portable film camera. It captured a series of 12 frames on one piece of film, and it's a beautiful image, but this is not 12 individual frames. It's not motion picture, it's a picture of motion.

The person many people now credit as having first pioneered perforation is our old friend from the Connaught Rooms, William Friese-Greene. By 1891, he was working a pinwheel perforation system on 60mm film using round holes. But the credit for this was almost entirely posthumous. Were it not for the dramatic manner of his death, he might have been completely forgotten by the British film industry which, the minute he was cold, finally celebrated him.

The truth of the story seems to be that his life was even sadder than his death. In 1889, he first patented his film camera, which took ten photographs per second on celluloid film strips. The result was imperfect and Friese-Greene, an obsessive dreamer of the highest order, ran himself aground, declaring bankruptcy in 1891 which forced him to sell his rights to the invention. At the expense of his career, finances and family, Friese-Greene continued to innovate unsuccessfully in the field. He had tried to create stereoscopic moving images to little result and spent his latter years developing a workable but unrefined process for creating colour films. A great mind, but a sad story. He would be canonised by the industry in the all-star biopic film *The Magic Box*, directed by the legendary John Boulting, starring Oscar winner Robert Donat as our hero and marketed with the valid claim "Over Sixty British Stars" (Richard Attenborough, Laurence Olivier, Michael Redgrave and Sid James to name but a few), The movie went on to eerily echo its subject matter by being a financial failure.

Back in Edison's lab, however, Dickson was making perhaps the most significant technical choice in film history: he created the bedrock film format – a strip of perforated film, 35mm in width, with four perforations on each side.

Until the recent moment that feature film production finally tipped towards digital, this would globally become absolutely the standard format for recording and projecting the moving image for over a century.

In August 1889, Edison visited the Exposition Universelle in Paris. There he might have seen Charles-Émile Reynaud's Theatre Optique, a complex innovation on the magic lantern which required a band of painted gelatin plates to be pulled mechanically past a light which projected through them. He also might have seen Ottamar Anschütz's Electrotachyscope, which used an intermittent light to highlight each individual image brought before it - the shutter effect - which would come to define original motion picture technology. Whether he observed these displays or not, by the following month Edison was ordering photographic roll film from the Eastman company and Dickson was cutting and perforating it.

Precisely how much Edison's meetings and observations of other people's work fed directly back to Dickson and the development of the Kinetoscope, we might never know. It is, however, fair to say that the principles the machine were built on had largely already been developed elsewhere. What Edison had over everybody else, however, was money, labour and commercial nous.

Although he is often credited as the father of cinema, Edison's Kinetoscope was still a couple of steps away from what we now recognise as the cinematic experience; it played only to an audience of one and it was not, strictly, a projection. The Kinetoscope was a sturdy sealed wooden box with a viewing window at the top. Inside, a reel of 35mm celluloid film was dragged past an electric light through a high-speed shutter system, giving the viewer the experience of watching the perfect moving photographic image.

In January 1894, a few months before the Kinetoscope launched to the public, Edison received the first ever U.S. copyright for a motion picture. The motion picture was actually not intended to be shown as such but was produced as a series of sequential images to accompany an article about the forthcoming technology in *Harper's Magazine*. Filmed in Edison's legendary Black Maria studio, America's first officially copyrighted motion picture was a five second sequence of Edison employee Fred Ott taking some snuff and sneezing.

The first Kinetoscope parlour opened in New York on April 14th 1894 at 115 Broadway to immediate success: ten machines, each showing one of the Kinetoscope company's catalogue of ten short films. The Kinetoscope Company was open for business the sales of machines and films brought in a profit of $85,000 in the first 11 months alone.

In a slightly strange sideways step, outside the auspices of his employer, Dickson worked with his friend Herman Casler on what he considered an improvement on the Kinetoscope.

Frustrated by the picture quality on his initial invention, with Casler he went back to stage one and created a machine that, rather than depending on film technology, advanced the capabilities of the humble flip book. With its large reel of hand-cranked sequential images, the Mutoscope went on to great success and was featured side-by-side with the Kinetoscope in nickelodeon parlours across the world. It benefitted from a much larger image area, with the films shot on a 68mm film and printed on to cards. Mutoscopes were still being manufactured in 1949 and became an early outlet for pornography. In the UK, they are still better known as 'What The Butler Saw Machines'.

A pair of Greek florists, Demetrius Georgiades and George Tragidis, who had a flower shop on Columbus Avenue in New York, rolled the dice and bought some Kinetoscopes. Seeing an opportunity to be the first to exploit this new technology in Europe, they quickly shipped them to France, setting up the first public exhibitions of the machines outside the U.S. Learning that Edison had failed to patent the Kinetoscope in Britain, they hot-footed it to London's Hatton Garden where they met the young instrument-maker Robert W. Paul and convinced him to take one of their machines apart to replicate it. He did so, and after delivering their order, quickly got into the business of manufacturing Kinetoscope knock-offs himself.

This was the entry point to Paul, who would go on to become arguably the first pioneer of British film. Since Edison controlled the film prints which the Kinetoscope depended on, and also held the British patents for the camera they were filmed on, Paul was forced to innovate. Teaming up with photographer Birt Acres, they used the Kinetoscope to reverse-engineer their way to the Paul-Acres Cinematograph Camera. With this camera, Paul set out and made his own films to display in his bootleg Kinetoscopes. In October 1895, a patent was filed by Paul to create a public spectacle. Inspired by H.G. Wells's *The Time Machine*, he wanted to create an entertainment in which people could experience traveling through time and space. Various methods would be employed to achieve this and one of them would be the projection of Kinetoscope films onto a screen. The idea never came to be but Paul was on the path to working out how the projection of Kinetoscope films onto a screen might, in itself, be quite the form of public entertainment.

So, do we now have our first motion picture as we know it today?

Actually, no. We already had that, and herein lies one of the strangest stories in the development of the moving image. In Leeds, England, on the 14th October 1888, a French-born artist/inventor called Louis Le Prince used his patented Single-Lens-Combi-Camera-Projector to shoot 2.11 seconds of footage on a paper-based photographic strip. The footage shows two women and two men walking, almost dancing, about in a garden. Now known as *Roundhay Garden Scene*, it is officially recognised as the oldest surviving film in existence. But it's only fairly recently that Le Prince has received this begrudging acknowledgment and his story is frustratingly muted in film history. Working quite independently from the more noted pioneers of film, it has been pretty well proven that Le Prince cracked single-lens filming first – Roundhay and Le Prince's short film of a bridge in Leeds pre-date *Monkeyshines No 1* by some 8 months. By 1889, Le Prince had discovered celluloid and was both filming and successfully projecting the moving image. The thing is this; he didn't demonstrate his invention in public. He was ready to. He planned to unveil the recorded and projected image in New York in September 1890. He had the venue booked and the equipment ready. In the preceding weeks to this, Le Prince had visited Dijon to see his brother

Albert and claim his share of the inheritance from their mother's estate. It was a lot of money and Le Prince needed money as he was deeply in debt. His brother claims to have put Le Prince on the train to Paris following their visit. Le Prince was never seen again.

There has been much speculation as to what might have happened to Le Prince. His family felt it might have been foul play on Edison's part – Le Prince's patent looked likely to thwart his own and a dead man's family would have no claim over it for seven years. The notion of an Edison-hired hitman seems unlikely because Edison didn't play that way – there are no other recorded instances of quite such foul play. He leaned more towards litigation and the application of copious legal funding. Some people believe it was Albert Le Prince who might have killed his brother, perhaps over the inheritance. Many people, however simply believe that Louis Le Prince, a man of pride, disappeared himself due to the embarrassment of his debt or the mental anguish caused by the pressure of being the first to bring his motion picture technology to the world. We'll never know. But the two things we do know are that, firstly, Le Prince was the first person to successfully film and project in the manner we now recognise as cinema and, secondly, everyone thinks it was The Lumiere Brothers who hold this honour.

We're told that history is written by the victors and film history seems not to be immune to this rule. Before we look at the legendary Lumieres, let's take a moment to at least namecheck those they outran.

Wordsworth Donisthorpe (co-founder of the British Chess Association and noted anarchist) who, as early as 1876 had filed a patent for his Kinesigraph film camera and, with his cousin W. C. Crofts in 1889, had patented a camera of the same name with which they successfully captured a 10-frame moving image of London's Trafalgar Square. They also patented a projector but appear not to have demonstrated it publicly.

There's Henri Joly, the perpetual almost-ran of early cinema, whose attempt at developing a Kinetoscope that could be enjoyed by up to four people at once – the Photozootrope – proved to be a damp squib. He would go on to create workable but commercially unsuccessful methods of eliminating flicker from projected images, creating a perception of depth to the moving image, and synchronising motion picture projection to phonograph sound. He was brilliant but never the winner of a race. His own film camera technology was funded, and ultimately appropriated by Charles Pathe, a name which still resonates in the modern film industry, whilst Joly died unrecognised, a 79 year-old night watchman in Paris.

Herman Casler and Henry Marvin worked with W.K. Dickson once he left Edison in April 1895 to develop their projector, the Biograph, which, largely to avoid Edison's firmly-held patents, utilised a huge 68mm film format and a friction, rather than sprocket system, to advance the film through. Their company, which advanced in name from The American Mutoscope Company to the American Mutoscope and Biograph Company to The Biograph Company, went on to be a film studio to be reckoned with, bringing the world such names as D.W. Griffith, Mary Pickford, Lionel Barrymore and Lillian Gish, but Casler and Marvin remain obscure names outside of academia.

Jean Aime LeRoy is either the true underdog or the untrustworthy scallywag of this era. His claims that he projected two Kinetoscope films to a New York audience in Riley's Optical Store on 5th February 1894 would have won him the crown could they ever have been substantiated. He filed no patents and the films he claimed to have screened had not been produced by the date he claimed to have screened them. There are theories purported to explain the inconsistencies in his story but any evidence appears to have been lost to time. Could his claims be proven, would he now hold the Lumiere's spot in the heart of film lovers everywhere? Probably not. He wouldn't have been the only one to beat them.

Rarely discussed are the Skladanowsky Brothers, Max and Emil, whose film projector, the Bioscop, was unveiled with a screening of short films to musical accompaniment before a stunned paying audience at the Wintergarten theatre in Berlin on November 1st 1895. This public showing of the projected moving image predates the Lumiere's by almost two months but is largely forgotten by history. To add insult to injury, the Skladanowskys had a booking to perform their film show in Paris starting in January 1896 at the Folies Bergere but were unceremoniously cancelled in favour of the Lumieres. Was this the first time a projected photographic film was displayed to a paying audience? Not even.

In September 1895, Thomas Armat and Charles Francis Jenkins projected films for a public audience. They held screenings of some of Edison's Kinetoscope films on their Phantoscope projector to visitors of the Cotton States Exposition in Atlanta. Unlike the thrilling blurry motion mess of the Kinetoscope's continuous motion, the Phantoscope would pause on each individual frame at a speed of around 10 frames per second, which gave a much clearer moving image. Arguments and court battles between the two men derailed the project. Eventually Armat would own the patent, which he sold to Edison who essentially renamed it the Vitascope and claimed it his own invention, with which he eventually graced the stage of projected film in 1896. Jenkins would go on to make his name as one of the great pioneers of television technology. So, were they, in fact, the first to have held a public film screening? Again, no.

On May 20th 1895, Woodville Latham and his sons Grey and Otway, owners of a Kinetoscope parlor in New York, projected films of a boxing match to a non-paying crowd. They were assisted by the secret help of that sneaky scamp W.K. Dickson and his Edison colleague Eugene Lauste to develop the Eidoloscope – a film projector which finally translated the

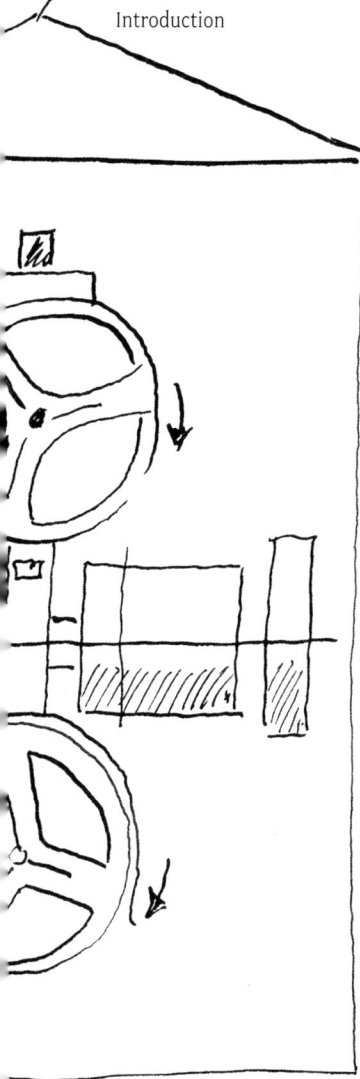

individual Kinetoscope viewing experience into an audience entertainment. It would appear that they were the first. But they are rarely represented as such. The Latham name is not entirely lost to history as it now belongs to the 'Latham Loop' - the loop of film utilised in cameras and projectors to this day which ensures the film tension is not too tight and allows films to be shot or projected continuously over long periods of time. Dickson claimed that it was actually Lauste, rather than a Latham, who invented the Latham Loop.

Finally, we arrive at the Lumiere brothers. Auguste and Louis, eldest sons of photographer Charles-Antoine Lumiere. Lumiere Senior moved into the production of photographic plates, opening a small factory in Lyon. Often veering towards bankruptcy, the boys were his saviour, devising newer, more sensitive photographic plates and the automated machinery required to manufacture them in high volumes. The company swelled to the degree that they were able to build a factory in Monplaisir and employ around 300 people – many of whom would collectively go on to stake their own place in film history.

In 1894, Antoine saw one of Edison's Kinetoscopes and it was obvious to him that his boys could equal, if not better, the contraption. With their curiosity piqued, Auguste and Louis had a working prototype of their Cinematographe within just a few months. Not only did this little wooden box pioneer the 'claw' mechanism still used today for advancing film strips through such machines, but it also was a wonder of economy in that the single device was a camera, projector and printer all in one.

The brothers did not want to premiere their creation in Paris at the time they did, they didn't think the technology was ready yet. It was Charles-Antoine who insisted upon it. And so it happened. The first show was for journalists, theatre owners and invited guests – including Méliès – and the subsequent 20 shows per day were for the paying public.

The programme was 15 minutes long and featured 10 films, the first of which showed the workers leaving the Lumiere factory at the end of a day's work.

So why are the Lumiere Brothers forever credited as being the first to bring film to the masses? The simple answer is because the Grand Cafe happening was one of actually two significant demonstrations, the first of which renders them bookends to this feverish handful of months. Although, with their legendary public screening on the 28th December 1895 in the basement of the Grand Cafe in Paris, they were pipped to the post by several competitors, they had previously held a very successful private demonstration for an extremely credible private audience of 200 on the 22nd of March that year at the Société d'Encouragement à l'Industrie Nationale (Society for the development of the National Industry). This conference was concerned with photography rather than cinematography and Louis Lumiere was surprised that his moving image work attracted more

chatter than the displays of the advances in colour photography.

At that moment in history, film was a novelty. The sheer thrill of seeing real life moments recorded and allowed to dance out repeatedly across a screen in a darkened room was entertainment enough. The films the Lumieres made and showed were documentary in its truest form; workers leaving a factory, a man hilariously failing to mount a horse (believe me, not as funny as it sounds), a baby playing with a bowl of goldfish, the delegates of the Congress of Photography in Lyon disembarking from a boat, a pair of blacksmiths at work, a mother and father feeding a baby, a man gymnastically jumping into a blanket, a street scene from Lyons and footage of boys jumping off a pier into the sea. Real life, magically captured. Only one film in the programme was staged and is widely viewed as the world's first comedy film. A gardener waters his garden, while unbeknownst to him a young boy steps on the hosepipe to stem the flow of water. When the gardener checks the nozzle, the boy jumps off and the old man gets a blast of water in the face. The gardener then catches the boy and spanks his bottom.

One might wonder if this was the film which captured the imagination of Méliès. The possibility for artifice and storytelling and entertainment derived not just from the medium but from the stories the medium was able to convey.

The Lumiere's tenure in the world of cinema was a short one: once the cinematographe had been superseded they spent the remainder of their career mainly concerned with their true passion – still photography.

Despite their refusal, after the show, to sell Méliès a Cinematographe of his own, the Lumieres that night handed him the baton which allowed cinema to pass from science to art (although the two remain forever entwined). Within four months, Méliès was exhibiting his own films in his own theatre and this is where our story ends. And begins. ★

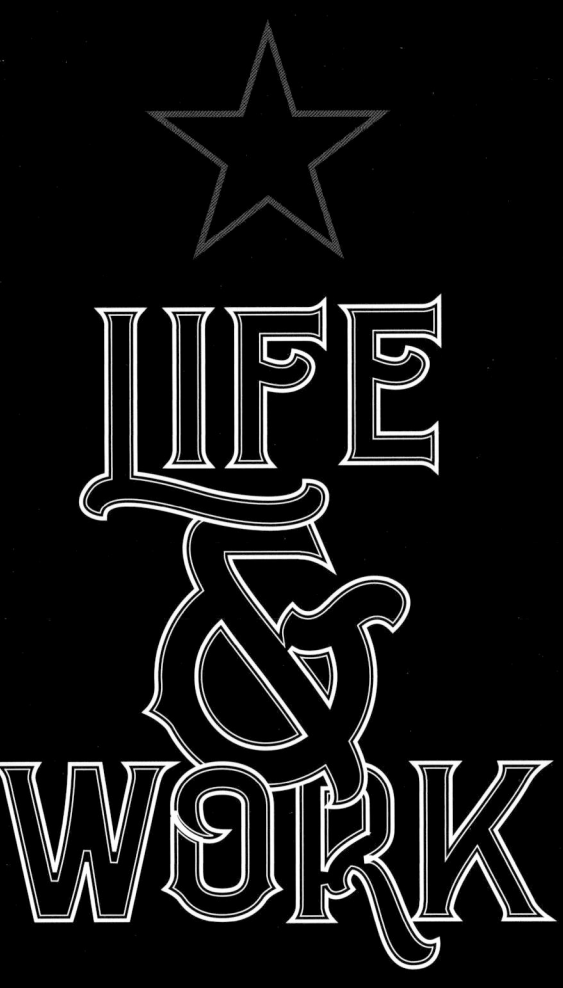

An Introduction to the Following Text

This autobiography originally appeared as a supplemental material in the book *Georges Méliès Mage*, a 1945 publication authored by Maurice Bessy and Lo Duca.

Bessy was something of a man-about-town in French cinema history. Starting as a journalist, he also became a novelist, a screenwriter, a film distributor, a film historian and collector and was appointed General Delegate of the Cannes Film Festival in 1971, for which he is credited with overhauling the selection process. Bessy had great working and personal relationships with many filmmakers. He was a close friend of Orson Welles and translated a couple of Welles's novels into French.

Joseph-Marie Lo Duca was an Italian-born art-critic and writer based in Paris. There, he was a founder of the Musee Canudo at the Palais de Chaillot to house the collection of important historical film ephemera he had amassed. In 1951, he co-founded the hugely influential magazine *Cahiers du Cinema* with Andre Bazin and Jacques Doniol-Valcroze and thereby became one of the principal architects of the Auteur theory. His involvement with cinema was multifaceted and he is notorious in some circles as the man who took it upon himself to re-edit, to his own taste, the only surviving negative of Dreyer's groundbreaking silent film *The Passion of Joan of Arc* – much to Dreyer's chagrin.

One of the most significant aspects of this document is that it has been written in the third person. This can be frustrating. More than this, as we see in the opening, Méliès not only refers to himself in this tense, but also seemingly takes on the role of an interviewing journalist. This led to some initial confusion on my part but, having compared the printed text to the manuscript that is clearly written in Méliès's own hand, I can confirm that this is no mistake. Why would Méliès do this?

Context is important.

When *Mage* was published, it described itself on the cover page as:

MAURICE BESSY et LO DUCA
GEORGES MÉLIÈS
MAGE
et
"MES MÉMOIRES"
par
MÉLIÈS

The limited edition version houses the manuscript facsimile in a pouch mounted to the rear inside cover with the words "Mes Memoires" printed on it. My Memoirs. I've found no record of Méliès ever referring to this document by this title. The title he gave it, as written clearly at the top of the manuscript, is *La Vie et L'oeuvre d'un des Plus Anciens Pionniers de la Cinematographie Mondiale Georges Méliès, Creatour du Spectacle Cinemtographique* which translates as *The Life and Work of One of the World's Earliest Pioneers of Cinema, Georges Méliès, Creator of Film as Spectacle.* This sounds even more braggadocious than the more humble "My Memoirs" but it shows perhaps a clearer view of how Méliès himself regarded this document.

When we think of an autobiography now, we see it as a published testimony from the writer to their readers, a summation of their life presented to the world for posterity. What became Mes Memoires was never intended to be this. Méliès didn't write this for us. In fact, the route to it ending up as part of Bessy and Lo Duca's book about him is slightly strange. His great-granddaughter described it to me as:

"In 1933, a French journalist asked Méliès to write his Memoirs. Then this text was sent to Italy in 1936, because the League of Nations had instructed Italy to publish a Dictionary of Illustrious Men. Italy was excluded from the League of Nations after it had invaded Ethiopia. This manuscript was however published by the Italian magazine 'Cinema' in 1938. Then in 1940, this magazine sold the manuscript of the Memoirs to Mr. Lo Duca, who became the owner of the papers (but not of the copyrights)."

So perhaps this is Méliès merely seeking control of his own reputation. Conceivably, by writing in the third person it denies the journalist who requested it the opportunity to put their own perspective upon it and maybe Méliès is hoping that by providing it as a fully written piece it will be published as such, rather than used as the basis for somebody else's interpretation of his career. If this is the case, there is an irony to the decision because, at least to modern eyes, the piece at times reads, in the third person, as fawning and obsequious.

Whatever the reason, there is so much to be learned from the study of a person referring to themselves in the third person on the understanding that they will not be revealed as the author of the piece. I suspect that many of us in Méliès's position would behave similarly – portraying ourselves in the best possible light, according ourselves the greatest honours and airing the injustices and misinterpretations of our work and legacy – yet Méliès, as with everything else he did, elevates this to an art form.

A quick note: Méliès regularly uses the terms 'Cinematograph', 'Cinematographer' and 'Cinematography'. It should be understood that these terms have a different modern interpretation, a Cinematographer now being a Director of Photography and Cinematography their craft. When Méliès describes himself as a Cinematographer, this should be interpreted as 'Filmmaker', Cinematography being the craft of Filmmaking and a Cinematograph is the camera he was using. ★

The Life and Work of One of the World's Earliest Pioneers of Cinema, Georges Méliès, Creator of Film as Spectacle

In this opening section, the very first thing Méliès seeks to do is portray himself as a humble man (or, more accurately, a humble "King") who would rather not be interviewed at all but eventually acquiesces for the good of film history. It would be easy, knowing that he is the author, to take an immediate dislike to the man on the basis of this paragraph alone. I urge you not to. Like all people who speak the highest of their own talents and achievements, you have to look behind the words and question the motives for their uttering. More often than not, such braggadocio covers deep insecurity.

At this time in his life, a year before his death, at the age of 75, Méliès was almost an archaic figure. Cinema had evolved. It was no longer silent, the people on the screen were no longer anonymous players but the most recognisable faces in the world. Hollywood was firmly established as the firmament of the industry and the industry was huge. In his final years, Méliès had experienced an affectionate swell in reputation – he was awarded the French Legion of Honour, which was the highest award the country could bestow upon him. He had also been honoured by a gala retrospective evening of his work on 16th December 1929 at the Salle Pleyel in Paris. A film enthusiast, J-P Mauclaire, had found a collection of 12 original Méliès film prints. They were damaged, but eight of the films were restored to new prints and shown on the night. However, eight out of over five hundred films barely represents a legacy. Méliès had fallen upon hard times since he left the world of film and had spent his final working years running a toy and sweet concession in the Montparnasse train station. His last six years were lived with his wife and granddaughter in an apartment within a retirement home for the film industry in Orly, funded by the Cinema Society. Although his contribution was recognised and celebrated amongst this new community – the film historians - it must have been frustrating and humiliating to Méliès that both his stature and his well-being depended entirely upon these people. Who could blame a man who had achieved so much and fallen so far for doing all he could to protect and bolster the reputation he would leave behind?

The life and work of one of the world's earliest pioneers of cinema, Georges Méliès, creator of film as spectacle

By Georges Méliès

Frequently beseeched from all sides to write his memoirs, Georges Méliès had always refused: "Nothing is more unpleasant and thankless," he would invariably reply, "than to talk about oneself and oneself exclusively". Nonetheless it was necessary, for *The History of Cinema*, to have a complete and authentic documentation of Méliès and his career. One of our collaborators sought to discover a way round this problem by paying a visit to the man himself, now in retirement, and by imploring him to provide us with the information we needed. He responded with great generosity: "This is completely different. Even if I don't wish to write my memoirs, I put myself entirely at your disposal to answer all your questions, from the moment that you find it appropriate, to clarify any historical details". Furthermore, thanks to long conversations with the man often referred to as 'The King of Illusion and Fantasmagoria', we are able to give a very accurate account of Méliès' considerable achievements, which opened infinite new horizons for cinema.

The Life and Work of One of the World's Earliest Pioneers of Cinema, Georges Méliès, Creator of Film as Spectacle

Méliès skips from his birth to his seventh year in the space of a single paragraph, leaving out important biographical information. He was born in Paris, the third son of a wealthy man. His father Louis had made his fortune in the manufacture of boots and shoes. Having been a traveling boot and shoe maker, he had fallen in love with Catherine, a co-worker at a boot factory where he was given work in Paris. Catherine was Dutch and her father was the bootmaker to The Hague. She married Louis in 1843 and they worked hard to build a business of their own.

Catherine and Louis had two sons before Georges-Henri (born 1844) and Gaston (born 1852). There was a gap of nine years before Georges was born on December 8th 1861. Catherine was 42 years old. Georges benefitted from his belated arrival, the family business had been built up and had brought wealth and property. Not only did Catherine have more time to spend upon and indulge him, the family also had greater means to provide him with the education his brothers had not received.

MÉLIÈS' YOUTH

In order properly to understand the particular circumstances which gave Georges Méliès the grounding that allowed him to carve out an unrivaled place in the history of cinematography, and to develop through this art an astonishing and even unique career, we must provide a few details on his youth prior to his first attempts at animated photography. Indeed, his innate taste for drawing, painting, caricature and sculpture, as well as an evident fondness for theatre, scenery and stage setting, can be traced to his childhood. It is these natural gifts, in addition to the various skills acquired little by little during adolescence, which later allowed him – once Louis Lumière's splendid invention had appeared – to produce the marvelous works which we know today.

Georges Méliès was born on the 8th of December 1861. Despite his age, he has retained his energy, enthusiasm, natural good humour and vivacity. If you were to express surprise to see him suffering so little the effects of age, he would laugh and reply: "I believe that the great workload and the numerous stunts required by many film shoots have the effect of preserving one's physical suppleness, since while art forms a significant element in cinema, there is also a no less important element of physicality, when it is not enough to watch others work but to get one's hands dirty and take risks for oneself. This isn't to say that it's a method of self-preservation, even if you don't kill yourself, which might occasionally happen, though that would be exceptional. Fortunately the truth is that most shoots pose no danger for the actors even if they can be exhausting beyond the imagination of those who don't appreciate what is involved."

The Life and Work of One of the World's Earliest Pioneers of Cinema, Georges Méliès, Creator of Film as Spectacle

Perhaps it was the stable background, comfortable future and encouragement of his family that left young Georges such a precocious talent. Lycee Louis-le-Grand, the school to which he was evacuated, was a notoriously bleak environment with an absence of warmth which likely made it the kind of place a creative child would distract themselves as much as possible with the cheerful refuge of art and fantasy.

At seven years of age he began his studies in classics at Lycée Michelet, in Vanves in the Paris region. At this time, the era of Napoleon III, this college was known as 'Lycée du Prince Impérial'. During the 1870 war, while the establishment was being bombed by the Germans, the pupils were sent to Lycée Louis-le-Grand in Paris, where Méliès continued his studies. He left school in 1879 and in 1880 went to Blois, where he undertook his compulsory military service. We point this out in order to refute certain articles in which younger cinema critics have labelled the pioneers of cinematography as 'primitives'; uncultured people incapable of producing anything of artistic worth. Méliès, by contrast, received a literary training, and even if early on he had to do what all cinematographers do (shoots which one might describe as 'ridiculous clowning', 'nonsensical farces' etc), this was purely due to the fact that the first cinema audiences were found at fairgrounds and composed of people who could only appreciate ludicrous pranks, crazy chases and reckless tumbling. Méliès' first reaction was to try to produce more thoughtful and artistic work, but at the time he came up against total incomprehension. Fortunately he was able to achieve his goals later, when the opening of larger theatres allowed him to reach a less 'primitive' audience, because it was indeed the fairground crowd and not the first cinematographers who might be thus described.

During his school years, while maintaining a respectable academic standard, Méliès was distracted by the demon of drawing, and though his grades were good he was frequently punished as a result of this passion for art. He was unable to help himself, and while he was preparing a French dissertation or studying Latin verse his pen would be involuntarily drawing portraits of his teachers or classmates, unless it was sketching a fantasy palace or an imaginary landscape which might already contain elements of a theatre set. His notebooks and even his textbooks thus found themselves highly illustrated. This was not at all to the taste of his teachers and earned him numerous detentions (he spent 11 years in boarding school). That's how to beat such ideas out of them! But it had no effect, Méliès continued to sketch and will sketch until his dying day!

Having gained his baccalaureat, served his compulsory military service (which his father might or might not have paid to have cut short) and spent some time in London, Georges returned home. He was keen to become a painter and, as he says, Louis denied him the chance to study at the Ecole des Beaux-Arts but what Georges doesn't note is that in exchange for his compliance, Louis did fund private art lessons.

It has been suggested that he was taught by the great Symbolist painter Gustave Moreau. If this is true, one could certainly detect a subtle influence in the work of Méliès – Moreau's work is full of winged women, stars, moons, suns, and in his 1876 painting The Apparition, a floating bearded head surrounded by celestial light eerily evokes the imagery Georges would go on to create on film.

Often his instinctive vocation for theatre drove him, barely 10 years old, to make puppets and decorations out of cardboard, which also brought him several punishments. When a little older, maybe 15 years of age, he would build puppet theatres to entertain his nieces. In short, he was gifted with great manual creative skills which he perfected day by day in small projects, each more complex than the last. All this would serve him well in years to come. When he had finished his military service, having always been top of the class in drawing and having already developed an aptitude for painting which he developed during his holidays, he returned to Paris with the intention to study at l'Ecole des Beaux-Arts and become a fine artist; but his father, a major industrialist, did not share his vision and vehemently opposed the idea, stating that anyone choosing such a profession could expect to starve to death. So, reluctantly, he had to join the family business. During his years there he was responsible for the factory machinery, its smooth running and repair, and it was there that he acquired the mechanical skills which would later be most useful in deciding his career path.

The Life and Work of One of the World's Earliest Pioneers of Cinema, Georges Méliès, Creator of Film as Spectacle

Méliès's first wife was Eugenie Genin: she, like his mother, was Dutch. Eugenie was introduced to the family through Georges's uncle and came with an impressive dowry. The fact that Georges does not mention her by name might be significant but what was definitely significant to him was that dowry. It allowed him to not work and concentrate on his new obsession – magic.

Nevil Maskelyne, the illusionist who had mentored Méliès in London, was somewhat of a figurehead. He had a 31 year long tenancy at the Egyptian Hall in Piccadilly, first with his partner George Cooke and then, following Cooke's death, with David Devant. Among Maskelyne's many achievements, his most enduring might be the invention of the pay-toilet door lock. Were it not for Maskelyne, we might never have had the term 'to spend a penny'.

Having developed a passion for Magic in London, Georges found himself a regular visitor in Paris to the spectacles on offer at the Theatre Robert-Houdin. Robert-Houdin had died 14 years earlier but still cast a hefty shadow over magic globally. A largely forgotten name outside of Magic now, his importance can be understood when we learn that the most famous magician in history – Erik Weisz – paid tribute to (or sought to capitalize on) him in his stage-name, Harry Houdini.

In 1885 he married, having spent the previous year in England in order to learn English. This was to be a great help to him. It was during his year in London that, not understanding enough English to appreciate plays, he took to frequenting the 'Egyptian Hall' managed by Maskelyne, an illusionist famous in England. It was a theatre devoted to magic, fantastical presentations and extravagant onstage illusions. After a while this assiduous attendance developed in him a great love for the art of magic; he studied closely this new area of theatre which complemented his artistic repertoire and, in two or three years, he became highly skilled in the art of illusion. Back in Paris he was a regular visitor to the Théâtre d'Illusions created by the great illusionist Robert-Houdin, perfected his skills and started to give performances, first of all in private, then at the Musée Grévan and in the theatre of Galerie Vivienne. Around the same time the 'monologues' created by Galipaux and Coquelin Cadet were causing a stir. Méliès also began to use this style in order to create variety in his show, and it was in this way that he started to learn the actor's trade. One can already see the range of knowledge which Méliès had acquired by the time he married at 23 years of age. He would later use all these skills in cinematography, with great virtuosity. But that isn't all. During this period he was also recognized as a journalist and illustrator, going by the name of Géo Smile in the satirical journal La Griffe, declared enemy of the famous General Boulanger who had almost overturned the French Republic and established a dictatorship in France. Had Boulanger succeeded, Méliès would at the very least have risked exile, as he had produced numerous lacerating caricatures ridiculing the brav' general, as his supporter the popular singer Paulus referred to him. This was to be Méliès' only incursion into the world of politics, which interested him much less than his artistic creations and inventions.

The considerable wealth which Méliès had acquired stems from the retirement of his father Louis in 1888. Louis gave equal shares of the business to his three sons and Georges gladly sold his share to his brothers. It has been suggested that Eugenie's money was also needed to buy the theatre outright. The term 'theatre' might be misleading as it was really just a room on the first floor of a building. It measured 17 metres long by 6 metres wide and seated just over 200. The name itself is also slightly misleading. The Great Robert-Houdin never once performed there. Ownership eventually passed to his son, also a magician, Emile Robert-Houdin, who also didn't perform there. When he died, it was his widow who sold the theatre to Méliès and it wasn't as prestigious a venue as it might have sounded. Despite being equipped with incredible technical machinery to assist any illusionist with ambition, the theatre struggled to compete with Paris's larger and more grandiose venues. It would be a decade before it turned a profit for Méliès.

In 1888 the Théâtre Robert-Houdin came up for sale. Georges Méliès, who had already acquired considerable wealth, bought the establishment, refurbished and transformed it, and there began his career as a maker of theatrical props, set designer and illusionist. He maintained the management of the theatre for over 36 years and created numerous illusions. The Théâtre Robert-Houdin was demolished in 1923 to allow for the completion of the Boulevard Haussmann, following 74 uninterrupted years of theatrical productions. Méliès was its last and longest-standing director.

The programme at the Theatre Robert-Houdin was varied and spectacular. Along with the expected Magician performances and grand illusions, there were also displays of automata – beautiful and intricate mechanical robots who could perform breathtaking functions. Méliès built these himself and they were truly impressive, although some of them were not truly automatic and depended on a little help from compressed air, electricity or cleverly concealed human operation. There were also Feeries – gorgeous staged fantasies, performed fairy tales with elaborate special effects, music and acrobatics. Méliès would be responsible for bringing this genre to cinema with his 1899 film of Cinderella. Among the staff and performers already in situ at the Robert-Houdin was one Fanny Manieux, an actress and regular participant of Méliès's onstage illusions. Her stage name was Jehanne D'Alcy. She would go on to appear in Méliès's films and, eventually, become his second wife in 1925.

The 'Molteni' lanterns Méliès references are better known to us now as Magic Lanterns. The Magic Lantern was very much the precursor to cinema. Hand painted glass slides with moving parts placed before an electric light source and projected onto walls produced entertaining animated images for audiences. Later on, photographic slides were also incorporated. The most arresting uses of the Magic Lantern were in the field of Phantasmagoria, horror shows utilising multiple lanterns, music and sound effects. The co-ordination in the execution of these displays had to be impeccable. Layers of elements were built up, often through rear-projection on several screens to terrifying effect. Méliès was quite the master of the art and elevated his work above the cheap scares and chattering skulls of many of his rivals. He took delight in creating the most beautiful, inventive experiences for his audience. As he states, this was also an incredible preparation for cinema. Much of the content, style and execution of his film work was rooted in this period. The Magic Lantern itself was pivotal in the progression of the artform as it was a Molteni that the Lumieres would use as the light source for the projection of their first film displays.

Méliès was keenly aware that the projected photographic moving image was on the way. In 1894, Jehanne D'Alcy had travelled to America and met the English engineer Robert Paul who had told her about the advances that Edison was making with his Kinetoscope. Paul made good money from his pirated version of that very machine and had developed his own camera with Birt Acres to produce their own film strips to be shown in their own machines. Méliès travelled to London to meet Paul and was impressed by his work but found no application for it yet as all of his own work was directed at a theatre audience. The Kinetoscope could not entertain a room of 200 people at once. He knew that projection was on the way, but this was not it.

During the 7 years following his arrival at the theatre, Méliès devoted all his time to it. The Chambre Syndicale des Artistes Illusionistes (the Illusionists' Guild) chose him as president and he would hold this position for 40 consecutive years, 4 more years than he stayed at the theatre. Cinema was yet to arrive. In December 1895 the first cinematographic presentation took place, and from early 1896 Méliès added the new role of film-maker to his many occupations. From this moment he embarked on a life of frenetic activity with little respite and which would continue for 20 years, until the outbreak of war in 1914. For several years, and well before animated film was considered an art, the shows at the Théâtre Robert-Houdin would regularly close with the projection of a series of photographic shots on coloured glass (most often on the subject of travel along with various hand-painted comical scenes, multicoloured chromates or rosettes rotating for attractive decorative effect). These projections were created by oxydric light by the use of several Molteni lanterns assembled in such a way that they allowed the melting of one scene into another. The process was the equivalent of the 'fadeout' in contemporary cinematography. Furthermore, the use of various mechanized plates allowed for a range of effects such as falling snow, lightning, day and night, the passing of cars on a road, railways, riverboats etc. This was all achieved by the use of horizontally sliding glass plates. It was, in fact, an update of the traditional magic lantern theatre which preceded cinematography. However, unlike those in cinema, the painted characters were immobile and would slide in simple fashion like the cut-out figures in Chinese shadow theatre. Despite this imperfection the public appreciated these projections because through them they saw remarkable photographs of unknown locations and countries, decorated in attractive colours. We must remember that this created a familiarity with the projections themselves, performed with either the oxyhydrogen lamp, with the oxyetheric lamp, or with electric arc lamps. From this particular point of view, Méliès' education was already complete when he entered into cinematography, which was for him a clear advantage, cinematic lighting machinery being absolutely identical, at least at this moment in time.

The article Méliès references here is an important one for him. Leon Druholt was the editor of Cine-Journal. For Druholt, it was something of a personal crusade to shine light on Méliès's important contribution and it seems that the rediscovery and canonisation of the man substantively began at this point.

Here Méliès gives a very succinct bullet-point summation of his own life and career as observed by Druholt. He will elaborate on this but right now seems caught up in the unique position of speaking in the fourth person about himself.

In this paragraph, Méliès skates quickly over an important period, which he will later elaborate on slightly more.

28th December 1895 has always been regarded as the epoch of film history. It was on this date, in the basement Salon Indien of the Grand Cafe on Paris's Boulevard des Capucines, that Louis and Auguste Lumiere unveiled their Cinematograph to an invited audience of around thirty-five, the grand reveal of the projected photographic moving image on film. It's interesting that Méliès claims to have been invited by Louis Lumiere to this hugely significant event. He has contradicted himself on this point. In an interview he gave several years later, he offers the more likely version that he was actually invited by Louis's father. Antoine Lumiere had a photographic studio in the same building as the Theatre Robert-Houdin. In fact, it was directly above. He and Méliès were friends and, in Georges's later re-telling of the events, his invitation was issued by Antoine in the stairwell of the building they shared on the day of the screening itself. Maybe a chance encounter and a last-minute invitation to the birth of cinema were not as fitting a tribute to Méliès than a personal invitation from one of the inventors themselves and subsequently needed to be rewritten. In my correspondence with Méliès's great-granddaughter Anne-Marie Malthête-Quévrain, she told me

"Méliès began a campaign among journalists and historians in 1925, as to explain his eminent role in the development of cinema, but at that time the films were lost in France, as well as the catalogs of his production, so he could write things in his own way."

This should be remembered whilst reading his words. They were written at a time in which personal testimony was unlikely to be scrutinised, and so a certain elevation of one's perception might be forgiven. That said, it's a mark in his favour that he quickly admits to vexation when the Lumieres refuse his offers to rent or buy their device for use in his theatre.

It was not one month until Méliès would begin to show films at his theatre, it was not until the 5th April 1896 that he would do this. In between the Grand Cafe screening and this date, Méliès would travel to London to buy one of R.W. Paul's 'Animatographs' (sometimes known as the Theatrograph), the first commercially produced film projector. It is possible that Méliès purchased this from fellow magician-filmmaker David Devant. Paul had unveiled his creation in a presentation at the Finsbury Technical College on the 20th of February 1896. Unfortunately for him, the Lumieres were also in London that day and gave a more prestigious presentation of their own (markedly superior) kit at the London Polytechnic on Regent Street. The lecture theatre in which they put on their show has recently reopened to the public as The Regent Street Cinema: it has been fully restored to its original architectural beauty and is a powerful place to sit for those excited by film history.

Below we present an extract from a record of Méliès' cinematographic activities, which appeared in Ciné-Journal under the name of Léon Druhot, to allow us a glimpse of his work.

"Georges Méliès has just, at the request of the Corporation, been named chevalier de la Légion d'Honneur (the French equivalent of a knighthood). This is only fair, but how late is justice delivered for one of the earliest and most important pioneers of cinematography!"

Let's take a look at the stages of Méliès' extremely prolific life:

In 1895, at the invitation of Louis Lumière, he witnesses the first cinematographic screening (known as the 'historical session') and is amazed by the sight of the first animated photographs. He wishes to buy or rent such a machine for his theatre, but Lumière refuses to sell... Frustrated, Méliès – having seen an instrument capable of producing a superb spectacle for his theatre – seeks and collects components, and builds for himself his first camera and, one month later, projects his first films and opens, in the Théâtre Robert-Houdin, the world's first public cinema.

In October 1896 he builds, in his property at Montreuil-sous-Bois, the first cinematographic studio with a stage and theatrical props.

In 1896 he creates the cinematographic spectacle itself, by presenting the first great plays and the first historical re-enactments.

From 1897 onwards he invents successively the processes of 'rigging' that have subsequently become universal and continues to develop cinematographic technique with his inventions.

In 1898–99 he creates the ferric or fantasmagorical genre, having successively instigated all the other cinematic genres: drama, comedy, vaudeville, opera, comic opera, operetta, open-air shoots, films of fantasy journeys, documentaries, cine-reality etc.

In 1900 he establishes the first Chambre Syndicale des éditeurs cinématographiques (Cinema Directors' Guild). The meeting place is the foyer of the Théâtre Robert-Houdin, 8 Boulevard des Italiens. Elected president, he fulfills this role until 1912.

Méliès purchased the Animatograph and some short films, some by Edison, some made by Paul himself, who would go on to produce almost 1000 films in the next decade or so. His earliest success was an 1895 film shot for his Kinetoscopes called Rough Sea at Dover which, when projected, was a very dramatic sight for those not yet used to projected film.

Maurice Noverre has been credited as the first film historian. He was a passionate character who seemed to regard the early pioneers of cinema as the true underdogs of the industry and spent a lot of the time being vocal on the subject. He was a true champion of Méliès and his description of Méliès's achievements here is irrefutable. He fought even more passionately on behalf of Emile Reynaud, inventor of the Praxinoscope, to be recognised as the true progenitor of cinema but was unsuccessful in this.

In this final paragraph, it is very possible Méliès has ascended to the use of the fifth person in that he is, in the third person, quoting a letter that he himself has written. The ability to talk in the fifth person is perhaps his most criminally overlooked achievement. I feel proud to be able to finally shine a light on this.

In 1908 and 1909 he chairs the first two Congrès Internationaux du Cinéma, France, Italy, England, Germany and USA being the only nations to regularly produce films at this time. Despite the determined resistance of all the production studios who had refused point blank to change their working methods, he convinces them of the necessity of unifying perforation, succeeding and thus ensuring the sustained growth of the international film industry (Cine-Journal of April 17, 1909)

In 1904, in response to the copying and imitations of his films in America, he opens an office and laboratories in New York, under the direction of one of his brothers; this ensures, by issuing a copyright, respect for the ownership of his works. He is soon persuaded to join the 'Edison trust', which at that time claims all patents pertaining to cinematography and, as a result, having won his case, can demand royalties on the sale of films from other production companies. From this moment on, copies are made of all negatives in his Montreuil studio, and a set of negatives is dispatched to New York from which a positives are made for the US market, since the importation of positives from France would incur excessive taxation.

Illustrator, set designer, illusionist, scriptwriter, producer and artistic director of all his creations, he produces, from 1896 to 1914, a considerable number of films drawn entirely from his imagination. These films achieve worldwide success and earn him titles such as 'The King of Fantasmagoria', 'The Jules Verne of Cinema' or 'The Magician of the Screen'.

Despite an enormous daily workload, for 36 years he continues to manage the Théâtre Robert-Houdin in Paris, where he invents and constructs an endless number of props and illusions.

During the war in 1914 he establishes the Variétés Artistiques opera house in Montreuil. With his son, daughter and a troupe of Parisian performers he presents all the major works from the canon of opera, comic opera and operetta, as well as a number of dramas, vaudeville shows and comedies; this will continue until 1923. His daughter Georgette Méliès, an excellent operatic signer, and his son, a very amusing comedy lead, along with Méliès himself achieve great success as actors. Georges Méliès will play more than 98 very diverse roles in this theatre.

As a screen actor, far from limiting himself to one unchanging type, as so many famous actors have done, he always attempts to bring to life a great range of characters and to make himself unrecognizable through artful use of make-up. Moreover, he is never personally named in his programmes and posters. Only the title of the film appears in the opening sequence and we see no artists listed, contrary to contemporary practice. These films, conceived exclusively and specifically for the cinema, are also screened without subtitles in all countries, the scenarios being always very clear and cinema-oriented. During the era of silent film this is the perfect formula for international cinema. With this system no dubbing is necessary, whatever the audience's language might be – naturally enough!

Finally, having incurred great financial losses during the war, he finds himself, very reluctantly, forced to abandon the art which he had done so much to create. When all is said and done, Méliès can lay claim to the title 'doyen of all film producers, entrepreneurs, screenwriters, directors, set designers and actors'! What's more, without partner investors, he used only his own capital. How many filmmakers can say that?

We finish this overview of Georges Méliès career with this paragraph taken from an article by Maurice Noverre in Nouvel Art Cinématographique:

"In the creation of the cinema show, who first understood what could be achieved through cinematography? Is it not he who built the first studio; who first conceived and brought about great scenic innovations to replace the modest films shot from a distance of 17 metres; who created the various processes known as 'special effects'; who was the first to reproduce events from history, to bring to life mythological tales and scenes, to compose, stage and perform fairy tales; who created cinematic fantasmagoria and fantastic journeys; who brought to the screen drama, comedy, opera, comic opera, operetta; who designed and constructed the first cinematic sets; who gifted to cinema great costume dramas (from 1896 to 1914); who, ultimately, was the revelation incarnate of the infinite possibilities of the cinematographic art and the creator of current cinema? Georges Méliès is that man!"

Let's limit ourselves to this one citation. Endless articles have been written about Méliès, articles which tend to reaffirm each other and to recognise the influence which he had on the extraordinary success of the cinematographic art the world over.

Méliès makes an important point here – this era in which pre-cinema and early cinema crossover is not just a short one but an incredibly busy one with many players working independently on a global basis. Information sharing was rare as this was very much a race to perfect the process, patent and unveil it before anyone else had a chance. Had the Lumieres decided to take another few months to further perfect their system, somebody else would undoubtedly have pipped them to the post. To sort through all of the patents in all of the countries pertaining to movie cameras and projectors from this brief moment would reveal a lot of hastily stolen ideas and appropriated mechanisms. As soon as any piece of equipment decisively came to market, it would be bought, dismantled, rearranged and repatented by someone else, Méliès included.

Méliès's first films bore no similarity to the fantasies for which he would become famous. His first ever film, *Une Partie De Cartes*, or *Playing Cards*, is in fact an almost exact copy of Louis Lumiere's film titled *Partie De Cartes*. Both films show a card game and are photographed from a single static location, framed almost identically. Méliès's film *Arrival of a Train at Vincennes Station* is currently missing, but one could believe from the title (and a flipbook which some believe represents this footage) that it is a recreation of the Lumiere's *The Arrival of a Train at La Ciotat*. As he describes, at this time there were great limitations – specifically the inabilities of the equipment to hold enough film stock to shoot for very long and the expense of that film stock. There was also the lack of a supporting industry around these early filmmakers, particularly in regard to developing negatives and producing film prints for projection. To achieve his vision of what film could be, Méliès had to first perfect the technology, then devise and master the physical production processes. The early films were experiments, demonstrations of the technology. They were little more than moving photographs, but at that time to see a photograph move was almost inconceivable. Méliès himself wasn't entirely sure that film had life beyond this novelty. Once the illusion of movement lost its appeal, would audiences actually have any more use for this format? Méliès certainly wasn't initially fully committed to what would become cinema and the films were incorporated into his shows rather than being the total extent of them. This would soon change.

THE CINEMATOGRAPHER AND HIS EARLY STRUGGLES

In the details which follow we attempt to illustrate the great ordeals which the first pioneers of cinema had to overcome. Those who today seek to make motion pictures will find all the required equipment available, complete and perfected: all they need is the necessary funds. They cannot begin to imagine the difficulties against which the creators of this industry had to struggle, at a time when no such material yet existed and when each innovator kept their work and research a closely guarded secret. Therefore Méliès, just like Pathé, Gaumont and others, was only able to progress by making numerous machines, subsequently abandoned and replaced by others which were themselves in due course replaced. As one might imagine, this involved a great waste of time and money, which is why, during the first nine months of 1896, Méliès and others filmed only open air scenes or inconsequential short comic sequences. His time was taken up with the creation and refinement of equipment and methodology (photography, development, print and projection). When he finally had a well organized laboratory he was able to give free rein to his vivid imagination, and to begin the long series of extraordinary films which commenced in 1896 with *L'Escamotage d'Une Dame* at the Théâtre Robert-Houdin and which continued to astonish audiences until 1914. There followed works of increasing significance which would within a short period of time make their creator known throughout the world. There can be no doubt that in cinematic circles the GEO-MÉLIÈS-STAR-FILM brand which he created was held in great esteem for the virtuosity of its productions and for their international character.

The Life and Work of One of the World's Earliest Pioneers of Cinema, Georges Méliès, Creator of Film as Spectacle

It must have been a great frustration to Méliès that the projector he had bought from Paul did not measure up to the quality of the one the Lumieres were currently touring around the world to great acclaim. But, by installing the projector in situ at the Robert-Houdin, Méliès was the first person to create what we would now recognise as a cinema. This was the only place in the world in which film was neither a traveling novelty show or a fairground attraction.

Méliès, having been unable to acquire similar equipment, considered the situation and decided to build his own. Clement Maurice, Mesguich, Promio and Trewey were beginning to make cinematography, in the form of documentaries, internationally recognised, for example in England, Russia, USA and Germany. It was at this time that a stroke of luck came to Méliès' aid: he learned that the English optician W. Paul had just made available a projector which allowed the projection of films shot against a black background, on the Edison Kinétoscope. Under pressure to screen his work at any cost, he bought one of these machines and procured some Edison film reels, the only ones that he could find and in very limited number. It was with this rudimentary equipment that the Théâtre Robert-Houdin opened the first indoor cinema, in contrast to the makeshift fairground screenings of the new invention's first practitioners.

It wasn't long before Méliès announced a pause in his cinema show, due to his decision to rework Paul's projector into a camera he could use to make his own films. This might sound like a crazy idea now, but some of the early inventions were both cameras and projectors in one box, since the most important principle was being able – for both capturing and projecting – to crank perforated film through a gate one frame at a time. In one instance it was to expose the frame, in the other to project light through it. Méliès worked with Lucien Korston, a mechanic he knew and Lucien Reulos, who was an engineer capable of producing the new parts needed. The three men were named on the patent filed on the 20th of November 1896 for this new invention, named the Kinetographe. The machine itself was literally the one which had been purchased from Paul – it still has the serial number Paul himself put upon it – complete with custom modifications. It could be argued that Paul's name belongs on that patent too but since Paul's work in this field had been so largely appropriated from Edison, we see again that this was hardly an honourable moment. Still, Méliès has been accused of lessening Paul's contribution and claiming slightly more credit for himself than he might have deserved.

Studying the mechanical operation of this machine made Méliès realize that shooting could only be achieved through the use of a similar device; [the film was] enclosed in a lightproof box(a camera), equipped with a special lens for photography and different projection lenses. It was therefore based on the construction of W. Paul's apparatus that Méliès built his own.

An engineer of great precision, experienced in the manufacture of mechanical and automated devices that were displayed in his theatre, Méliès nonetheless experienced great difficulty in its construction. No replacement components, no turning cogs, no special lenses were commercially available. It was therefore necessary to build this camera from scratch, on slender means, in the little workshop of the Théâtre Robert-Houdin which was used for the construction and repair of automatons and magic devices. In February 1896, once the camera was finally ready, he found that by chance he had created, at the first attempt, a device quite different from the Lumière system, but completely satisfactory. It now only remained to make a number of trial shoots. Now the hard work really began. In Paris it was impossible to find the necessary virgin film. Learning that W. Paul had some in London, Méliès wasted no time in leaving for England, but faced with the optician's refusal to give him some 20 trial reels he found himself forced to acquire – for the at this time enormous sum of 45,000 francs – a whole box of virgin film from Eastman, without knowing if he would ever recover this investment. Who could have foreseen the success that cinema would go on to achieve? No one, without doubt, yet Méliès had faith in his instincts.

The Life and Work of One of the World's Earliest Pioneers of Cinema, Georges Méliès, Creator of Film as Spectacle

The film not being perforated would have been a massive problem. When you consider that each frame of 35mm film has 4 perforations and film runs at 24 frames per second, a device capable of punching just two perforations at a time would lead to a lot of work.

On his return to Paris a new challenge awaited him. The film brought from London was unperforated! Since all the cases were hermetically sealed this detail had gone unnoticed, but what a detail! There was no perforator, where and how could one be found? Only Edison had one. A certain Mr Lapipe, resident at 141 Rue Oberkampf, took up the challenge to construct an instrument for perforating film. Its rhythm was similar to that of military parade-ground drums, but what an instrument! In reality a hand-operated hammer, it was extremely difficult to manipulate and to make matters worse only made two holes at a time. It is not hard to appreciate the long hours required and the extreme fatigue which resulted. Using each hand alternately left the arms and shoulders demolished after 15 minutes.

The Life and Work of One of the World's Earliest Pioneers of Cinema, Georges Méliès, Creator of Film as Spectacle

It was however with this unlikely tool that Méliès perforated his first films and was able to make his first shoot. But he immediately came up against another problem. How to develop these long reels which were totally unlike the 13x18 or the 18x24 prints which, as an amateur photographer, he was used to developing in trays?

Who would have believed that in the early days Méliès, like his contemporaries, was reduced to cutting his films into sections in a bucketful of developer; then, still in the developer, joining them together; then joining together the longer sections after drying! What a time-consuming and delicate task to avoid scratching the gelatin or leaving fingerprints. Yet it is known that Méliès was ingenious by nature. He thus immediately undertook a test, wrapping one of his films around a large glass jar, each end glued with wax, and by soaking the jar in his bucket he had the satisfaction of seeing the development take place without endangering the images, calmly monitoring their emergence. Following this successful experiment, the next day he assembled semicircular shallow vats and wooden drums with hand-cranks that could turn inside them, similar to a cylinder for grinding coffee. This system worked wonders, and although most commercial developers later used industry standard frameworks, Méliès throughout his career remained loyal to his preferred original system. There were, in fact, several interesting advantages:

A small amount of developer in the bottom of the vat was enough to cover the entire film as it rotated.

As the liquid was constantly stirred by the rotation, no air bubbles or dust could stick to the film and damage the image.

The same roller moved the film into a vat of running water, the various stages passed quickly and the final wash was the most vigorous.

So the films passed across 1.5m drums which, electrically driven, produced a rapid turnover without staining, drops of water being driven out by centrifugal force. Subsequently the vats for development, fixing and washing would be powered entirely by electricity, and the drying rollers were fitted with an interior heating element, necessary particularly in winter. But in the beginning all was done by hand and, naturally enough, output was lower and fatigue infinitely greater.

Joseph Debrie was a Parisian engineer who had specialised in creating machines to cut sheet metal. In 1897, he was tasked by Méliès associate Lucien Reulos to create a machine for the perforation of film stock and is brought into the industry which will guide his future career. He becomes one of the leading forces in the world for the creation of automated machinery to support the film industry, building machines for printing, titling and developing film. Joseph brought his son Andre into the business and challenged him to develop a lightweight, portable film camera. The Parvo would go on to become one of the most significant film cameras of the era and remained in production for 50 years. Andre would remain at the cutting edge throughout his career. He even developed the camera equipment which Abel Gance would use to realise his three-projector/three-screen epic Napoleon. Andre died in 1967 but his company, now called CTM-Debrie still manufactures film equipment to this day.

For all of the self-aggrandising that this third-person tribute heaps upon us, it is quite simply a statement of fact. The processes that Méliès identified and created to produce what we now call 'special effects', along with his basic technical discoveries, undeniably place him firmly in the category of film genius. No other person discovered and implemented so many of the basic tenets of film-making as Méliès.

The development of his negatives completed, Méliès' troubles were far from over. He faced a long struggle to achieve the construction of machines for making prints which would produce satisfactory results. His early, flawed devices caused him endless troubles, and as is so often the case with inventors, it was the simplest idea that proved to be the best, coming to him after he had become bogged down in pointless and unsolvable complications. One can laugh about it now, but despite his natural ingenuity, he had to admit that he had not realized that the print-making machine was nothing more than a copy of the shooting mechanism, feeding through two films – the negative and the virgin positive – at the same time. Once he finally understood he managed to make a perfect printer, but this process of trial and error had cost him precious time and great expense for little return. (The inventor's life is not all sweetness and light!) Shortly afterwards Joseph Debrie perfected excellent printing machines, and from that moment on Méliès no longer took the trouble to build his own; he became, rather, a loyal client of this conscientious artisan who subsequently also provided him with a whole series of perforating machines, each one an improvement on the last. Joseph's son André Debrie continued to build all forms of cinematographic equipment, applying the same assiduousness and adding contemporary technical refinements.

THE TECHNIQUE OF FANTASY

It would nonetheless be a mistake to believe that Méliès, once he had finally created practical and efficient equipment, no longer had to overcome any difficulty in the production of his films. It is well known that, following the success of his lavish shows and special effects, he ended up specializing in cinematographic shots which presented the most extraordinary technical problems. Far from avoiding these problems, he took the greatest pleasure in researching them, cataloguing their apparent impossibilities and finding ways to resolve them. He thus achieved a virtuosity which has never been surpassed or even equalled. No one could doubt his great mastery in works of fantastical imagination.

Despite how frustrating the photochemical process was, Méliès was developing 'tricks' from quite early on. His first contribution was the 'stop trick'; During 1896, his first year of making films, Méliès was filming, near his office in Place de l'Opera, just filming a shot of the bustle of the street from a static position. The film jammed in the camera and it took him a minute to get the camera working again. He continued to film. This film no longer survives, but in later life Méliès described his 'eureka' moment as occurring whilst watching this film projected back. The film played continuously, yet at the moment of the jam, the street and buildings remained the same but a bus turned into a hearse and men turned into women. This was like magic to Méliès and magic was, of course, his stock-in-trade.

He would go on to pioneer the dissolve to provide a smooth transition between scenes, the matte shot, in which part of the lens is blocked so that the film can be wound back and then just that section re-exposed – allowing for a multitude of special effects including multiple exposure, which Méliès used with glee, allowing him to not just appear in his own films but appear many times within a single frame – interacting with all of his clones. He was also the pioneer of miniature and model work. It would take the best part of a century before these processes would be replaced by computers aping the very same effects.

The complex execution of these kinds of shots involves enormous difficulty at the printing stage. It is easy to understand why: today the vast majority of films are shot under artificial light, which allows shots of a richness that has become completely normal. The negative emulsions are also much more sensitive than those in the early days. The negative being therefore of high quality and consistent from across its whole length, there could be nothing easier than to obtain, via a mechanical press, regular and perfect prints. Once the speed is defined, according to the intensity of the negative, the printing of the positive takes its course from one end of the roll to the other.

The same could not be said of Méliès' shoots, made exclusively in daylight and which, due to the great complexity of their execution, could take a whole day to complete. The inevitable change in light caused by passing clouds resulted in highly inconsistent negatives, which came to be known as 'false hues'. To obtain more or less consistent positives from these negatives, which were in parts too pale and in others too dark, Méliès had to rely on a difficult and complex system. No other way was possible using these inconsistent negatives, the production of which involved a huge amount of work due to the special effects involved.

The Life and Work of One of the World's Earliest Pioneers of Cinema, Georges Méliès, Creator of Film as Spectacle

The hand-cranking mechanism which Méliès describes here, which featured in early cameras and projectors before they became motorised and the frame rate of 24 frames per second became standard, is something which was a curse of early cinema at the time and remains a curse today. The reason that early silent cinema often seems so quaint and unpalatable to engage with is that for so many years we saw it standardised to 24 frames per second and doused in sepia. To show a hand-cranked film at a rate different to that which it was filmed often means that everyone onscreen is moving comically fast. It looks stupid. At that time, camera operating was not just about composition and focus: it was about the subtle skill of cranking – if a scene needed to play fast, you'd crank it a little slower. If it needed to play slow, you'd crank it a little faster. It was all about rhythm and control. The same goes for projecting. The projectionist would need to understand the film and crank it sympathetically. Modern restorations of early films have righted this wrong to great effect but this comes too late for many consumers and silent cinema remains of niche appeal largely for this reason. Yet another way in which cinema differs from other art-forms whose earliest histories remain relevant and greatly respected.

Even if the process is repeated, similar faults appear elsewhere. It was therefore necessary to resort to an almost photographic process, dependent on the special effects and the performance being well executed. All these shots were then printed on hand-turned presses. A metronome in front of the operator set a rhythm for each turn of the handle. A sign accompanying each negative would carry information of the following kind: 1–25 normal speed; 25–41 less fast; 41–100 very slow; 100–150 very fast; 150–200 normal speed; etc. These speeds had been determined for each portion of the negative, after successive tests. The operator counted aloud (revolution counters did not yet exist) and was obliged to follow the instructions on his file with the greatest attention, forever varying the speed of the hand-crank and also, at times, the intensity of illumination. It was only through this sustained concentration that it was possible to obtain consistent results from inconsistent negatives. The sight of the press operators, appearing to turn the crank sometimes very fast and sometimes very slowly for no apparent reason, came as a shock to the rare laymen who were allowed to visit the laboratories; they wondered if the operators weren't just a little mentally disturbed.

What is most interesting for the reader is to witness the first infant steps of cinematography. We now return to the first camera built by Méliès. Still in his possession, this machine was truly a monument, of enormous weight and very unwieldy to transport. An oak box contained the mechanism which was itself mounted on a heavy cast-iron platform. The base of the machine was broad, cumbersome and heavy; a large iron wheel, attached to the feet of the tripod, added to its weight. By means of a leather strap it was used to manipulate a pulley on one side of the box, which set in motion the interior mechanism. This cast iron wheel, 0.5 metres in diameter, in combination with the small size of the pulley, produced a multiplication on the same principle as a bicycle pedal, translating to a speed of 16–18 images per second (a normal speed at this time). Today the image per second ratio is generally 24; when an older film produced at 16 images per second is screened at a speed of 24 the effect is faintly ridiculous: the performers move at an improbable pace and produce a comical impression.

Some of the fifteen 'views' he mentions here are "Unloading the Boat", "The Beach at Villiers in a Gale" and "Panorama of Havre Taken From a Boat", very simple scenic compositions yet here Méliès perfectly describes the frustration of achieving such simple results. The skill of loading unexposed film into a camera, although now slightly archaic in the digital age, essentially never got any simpler. It remains a bulky mechanical process in which one can not use one's eyes. To have achieved this alone, 20 times in a day, is no mean feat in itself.

There was a reason why Méliès made his machine so heavy. The vibrations from this primitive mechanism were such that considerable weight was necessary to ensure stability and counter the shaking induced by the iron wheel. Also, as far as its creator was concerned, this instrument was designed to remain in one place. It was not a portable device, but a workshop instrument which would allow, in secret and exclusively in the studio, the production of personal projects quite different from other contemporary productions. We have seen that Méliès was quite satisfied with the results obtained from this first camera, but quite apart from its enormous weight it also had the great inconvenience of being so noisy that its creator jokingly referred to it as his 'coffee grinder' or 'machine-gun'. To be fair we should recognize that most other early instruments had the same qualities. Nonetheless, after having filmed a number of comic or artistic routines in his studio, Méliès sought to arrange some maritime shots, in order to broaden his programme with open air scenes, or documentaries as they might today be called. So, boldly, he set out for Trouville and then Le Havre, laden down like a pack mule. These two days of work were terribly arduous. A storm was raging, because Méliès had chosen bad weather in order to obtain more dramatic results. His camera could only contain 20m of film, and could neither be loaded nor unloaded in the open air. He resorted to spending the day in improbably contortions, dismantling his equipment between each take and carrying it all to a photographer's studio to change film. He was alone and dared not leave anything lying around in case someone might touch his equipment… or even steal some of it. One can only imagine the exhaustion brought about by this routine, repeated 20 times a day and covering miles across sandy beaches where you might sink up to the knees under such a burden.

The Life and Work of One of the World's Earliest Pioneers of Cinema, Georges Méliès, Creator of Film as Spectacle

Yet it seems that Méliès' faith was unshakeable. He returned, worn out but triumphant, to Paris with some 15 films which had a profound effect on his audience. Such images had never been seen: the furious assault of the waves on the cliffs of Sainte-Adresse, the foaming of the sea, the drops of water projected into the air, the eddies, the sputtering spray. So many scenes, which would today hold no great interest, fascinated spectators used to the familiar theatrical representation of the sea produced by painted cloths with children crawling on all fours beneath them. What really amazed the audience was seeing, for the first time, a rigorously accurate reproduction of nature. Those who were familiar with the sea cried out, 'that's exactly what it's like!' and those who had never seen it had the sense that they were really there.

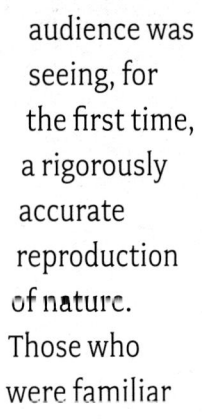

Since the camera had no viewfinder, the framing and focus had to be calculated as one would operate in photography, using a fragment of frosted glass. The framing, again as with standard photography, required a black cloth in order to block out daylight. In Le Havre the force of the wind was so great that, for all that Méliès clung on to his camera, he was unable to prevent the cloth from being torn off; he watched it fly away like a seagull, to some unknown destination. He never saw it again, of course, and collapsed into the sand along with his camera. No matter! What was it to Méliès, after all, to be chilled to the bone, wet through and bent double with fatigue? We know that his faith sustained him... and his films would be a success! How could he fail to be as happy as a king?

Méliès actually sold his Kinetographs to the public from a room in the Robert-Houdin but it was to be bested in the marketplace when the Lumieres made their Cinematographe commercially available. It seems Méliès fairly quickly realised that his energies would be better suited to film production. The speed with which technology was moving meant that newer, better cameras were constantly coming to market whilst film itself was now standardised at 35mm, meaning that Méliès could show anybody else's films on his equipment and vice versa. As he conveys here, Méliès was always a showman first and although he had the intellectual and operational nous to innovate technologically, his heart was more in inhabiting the grandiose descriptions that would be coined in his honour.

FILM CAMERAS AND OPERATORS PRE-1900

As soon as camera manufacturers began to appear, Méliès – who in the meantime had built the Kinetograph, a camera for amateur film enthusiasts – stopped working on the production of his machines, preferring to devote his energies exclusively to creating theatrical shoots. As film cameras became increasingly refined he used, in turn, Gaumont cameras with the Demeny system, Lumière cameras (finally commercially available), then Pathé cameras which were already much improved. From then on he was no longer troubled with the serious problems that had held him back early on, and he was able to devote himself entirely to technological progress and to the invention of a host of new and original methods of achieving special effects. Towards the end of his career, by using simultaneously well concealed theatrical props, certain conjuring techniques, all the photographic effects which he had discovered one after another, superimpositions, fade-outs of his own invention as well as pyrotechnic effects, he had managed to completely astound the most knowledgeable members of his audience, playing the role of the sorcerer who achieves the impossible with the greatest of ease. What can be said for sure is that, even now, several of his productions have left an indelible impression on those who witnessed their creation more than 30 years ago.

The Life and Work of One of the World's Earliest Pioneers of Cinema, Georges Méliès, Creator of Film as Spectacle

The first Kinetograph built by Méliès was unveiled in 1896; subsequent versions, constructed in sequence, were made available towards the middle of 1897. The device, which incorporated a very unusual drive system, was described in a brochure by Georges Brunel and was the first device to include a housing to protect the film from fire. In 1896 Méliès opened his first shop, at 14 Passage de l'Opera; he would then take over nos. 13, 16 and 17 as the laboratory was made larger to keep pace with growing demand. After the establishment in 1904 of the New York office which also contained laboratories for printing, in his Montreuil property already serving as his studio he installed laboratories bigger and more advanced than those at Passage de l'Opera; this would continue to operate until the declaration of war in 1914. From that moment he held a great advantage: he was able to develop his negatives as soon as a shoot was finished, to check the results, and to shoot the scene again if they were not satisfactory. Previously the printed negatives had to be taken to Paris for development, which meant that if the outcome was not up to scratch a second shoot would be necessary. This doubled the expense, as often substantial numbers of personnel would again have to be hired and paid.

The Life and Work of One of the World's Earliest Pioneers of Cinema, Georges Méliès, Creator of Film as Spectacle

A little more information on Méliès's camera operators: M. Leclerc had first been in Méliès's employ as a pianist at the Robert-Houdin. He would go on to co-patent a camera of his own – the Mirographe. He eventually left Méliès's employ after having been arrested for selling 'obscene' photographs. This was the moment Michaut got the job. Michaut, Lallement and Astaix left Méliès's employ in 1903 to form the distribution company American Kinema. L. Tainguy is presumably related to or another name for Méliès's business manager, who signed his correspondence P. Tainguy. Georgette Méliès was put to work early. Born in 1888, she was still a child when acting as both camera operator and projectionist for her father. She had appeared in his first ever film and would go on to a career in show business as a soprano singer.

At this point we should consider what is known about the camera operators employed by Méliès. He himself was operator on his earliest shoots; the first professional operator that he trained was Leclerc, followed by Michaut who subsequently, along with former Méliès employees Lallement and Astaix, opened the first film rental house. Then came L. Tainguy, who went on to work as an operator in New York, and finally Bardou. At this time, when it was necessary to operate two cameras simultaneously in order to obtain two similar negatives, it was Georgette Méliès who was the second operator alongside Tainguy and then Bardou. Méliès' daughter also operated the device which, on the mezzanine of the Théâtre Robert-Houdin, showed amusing publicity films every evening on the Boulevard des Italiens. This often involved advertising agents to bring a crowd who greatly enjoyed the films, though they also sometimes blocked the pavement. Inside, the screen operator was Calmels, the appointed engineer at the theatre, where he remained for 38 years and where he was in charge of projection for a period of 19 uninterrupted years until 1914. He was second only to Clement Maurice as operator of public screenings. As for Georgette Méliès, she was quite probably the first female camera operator and projectionist, as well as being one of the first female performers in cinema, in 1896, at 8 years of age. Her brother André, aged 3, also appeared in publicity films for Nestlé flour and Bornibus mustard! They were budding performers who would in due course make their own careers. Georgette, who sadly died aged 42, was an outstanding singer in opera and comic opera; her brother became and remains an excellent lead in operetta. Having started so young they both proved to be hugely talented artists.

Méliès was often involved in the machinations of the industry at large and was a respected figure but the industry was soon to change in ways irreparably damaging to him. The meeting he talks about here is a portent for problems to come. The notion of switching the market from a sales to a rental market came from Charles Pathe – probably the most dominant figure in cinema at that time and whose name and company remain important to this day. Pathe suggested that the standardisation of the market – cinemas renting prints of films for four months at a standard per-foot price, rather than buying them – was the way forward. This benefitted him greatly as he was capable of producing a large volume of cheap films and holding a vast share of the market. For an artist like Méliès, this proposal was nightmarish. His films were expensive to produce and laborious to make, his money was made from people buying his higher quality films at a higher price. He would be priced out of the market. The concern he went on to articulate was that the entire industry could be destroyed by such a move. There was still at this time a lurking fear within the industry that cinema might be little more than a fad, potentially prone to go the way of the Kinetoscope Parlor if the next thing that came along captured the public's attention. This paranoia has resurfaced throughout cinema's development. The advent of television was considered a huge threat, as was the dawn of home video and, now, we experience a moment in which Amazon and Netflix seem set to become the largest commissioners of feature films with no real need to ever screen their productions in cinemas. Here Méliès articulates what would go on to become the much vaunted "Showbusiness = Show & Business. Without the Show, you don't get the Business" argument, which continues to be relevant.

Let us now go back to the first International Congresses presided over by Méliès. We have seen that, in one of them, he had obtained unanimous assent for regularization of perforation throughout the world, an excellent outcome. Yet in another he had to undergo a Homeric struggle with a major publishing house which, up to that point, had obstinately refused to become part of the Chambre Syndicale des Éditeurs. This publisher, represented at the congress, claimed the right to impose a single price for the sale of films (at this stage films were not rented but sold by the metre). Méliès argued that this was an absurd way to operate, the price of a negative being entirely dependent upon the cost incurred in its production. By adopting this standard tariff they were preventing the growth and development of cinema, obliging producers to make cheap, mediocre films and limiting them to the employment of walk-on performers rather than recognized actors. As the discussion became heated, Méliès' opponent declared:

'You will never be anything but an "artist" and nothing more; myself, I am a businessman. This you will never be, because you fail to understand that in order to grow a business the most important thing is to have many clients, and to achieve this you have to sell at the lowest possible price!'

The Life and Work of One of the World's Earliest Pioneers of Cinema, Georges Méliès, Creator of Film as Spectacle

Méliès stood up and calmly replied: 'I am indeed just an artist, which in itself is quite something! But it is precisely because of this that I do not share your opinion. My belief is that cinema is an art, because it is the product of all the arts. Therefore cinema will either progress and refine itself to achieve greater and greater artistic worth, or, if by limiting its revenue it remains static and excludes any possible progress, it will very quickly founder! That is the truth of it. As far as I'm concerned, do not for one moment think that I consider being scornfully labelled an "artist" as a put-down, for if you, the "businessman" – and nothing more, therefore incapable of producing compositional films – did not have artists to make them for you, I wonder what you would be able to sell?'

This provoked great hilarity amongst those present; the argument was won and the 'prix unique' dispensed with as a result. Producers were free to make films according to their taste, and to sell them as they pleased.

Could it be possible to prevent the free competition which is indispensable to progress? Could those who sought to create ever be limited to producing works which were commercially viable but in themselves of no interest to the public? Fortunately, reason always wins out in the end.

Montreuil-sous-Bois was where Méliès lived. When his father had retired and left his business to his sons, Méliès had sold his share to his brothers for 500,000 francs, which would deem him a millionaire in modern terms. Along with acquiring the Theatre Robert-Houdin, Méliès had bought an estate with grounds and a house for his family. One of Méliès's ongoing frustrations with film production was that films really had to be shot outside to get the level of light needed to register a clear image. If you look at many early silent films, scenes set indoors often have a visible breeze blowing through the sets. The indoor sets had to be built outside. This meant that not only was the shoot subject to ever-changing natural light levels (a problem which can still plague a filmmaker even today) but it was also subject to the weather – a set could be destroyed by an unexpected rainfall. It was for this reason that in September 1896, Méliès began to build what we now recognise as the first film studio.

Edison had preceded the Méliès structure with a primitive but effective creation nicknamed the Black Maria. A Black Maria was a police van, the kind they threw suspects in when first detained to transport back to the station. It was nicknamed this – by William Dickson – because it was small, dark and uncomfortable. It was a woodframe building covered in black tar paper. In the roof was a large window, with which you could control the amount of light let in. The cleverest innovation of the Black Maria was that the entire thing was rotational, you could turn the structure around to best catch the sun at any time of the day.

Méliès designed and oversaw the construction of his studio, although he referred to it then as a workshop, entirely purpose-built to his needs. The main staging area was built to the exact dimensions of the Robert-Houdin, perhaps because he had grown so comfortable working within these confines, but the entire structure was built from iron and glass. Whereas the Black Maria could control light only from its roof and direction, the Méliès studio was entirely controllable. He initially built the frame from wood but the glass panels proved too heavy to maintain the integrity of the building. At considerable expense, he reinforced the structure with iron. This first phase of building gave him a workable space of 17 x 6 meters. The walls were four meters high and the tip of the roof which slanted either way from the centre was 6 meters. The entire building – walls and roof – was constructed from glass panels which could be covered by cloth when required. He had positioned the studio to face south-southwest as this gave the best front-light for the stage at 1pm each day. Méliès's workshop-studio would be emulated quickly by others and was the very prototype for the early film studio. When electric lighting and sound came in, film studios would become soundstages – large, dark spaces instead.

PERFORMERS IN CINEMA

Some details on the difficulties which Méliès encountered: at first, when he had the idea of setting up as a cinematographer in the field of theatre and showbusiness which would establish his lasting success, he came up against the refusal of actors to appear in his shoots. To them it was demeaning to work in a medium which they considered inferior and unworthy of their reputation. He had therefore, in his first films, to employ people who were willing but without any particular skill, and who were happy to perform the scenes which he described to them. (Actors subsequently completely changed their mind, competing for a role in films about to be made.) All the employees of the Théâtre Robert-Houdin, neighbours, family members, even domestic staff and the gardener, featured as actors and didn't do too badly. As for the extras, they were everyday men and women hired from the factories and workshops of the Montreuil neighbourhood. But alas! Despite their goodwill, the period costumes looked awkward on people who were not in the habit of wearing such outfits, and the poise of lords and ladies left something to be desired. The women in particular, even those who were otherwise physically attractive, lacked the elegance which comes with theatrical training. To sum up, they did not have the bearing, the flexibility in their gestures and gait, that indefinable quality of 'chic'. What to do? Méliès then had the idea of approaching the dancers at the Châtelet, who gladly accepted, being poorly paid at their theatre. From then on the female performers took on a quite different appeal. Having learned that the rates were good, in due course dancers from the Opera came to sign up in considerable numbers, followed by cabaret singers as well as other singers, by no means the worst, who saw the way things were going. Ultimately, as everyone in the world of theatre knows, the actors ended up saying 'hey, why should we miss out?' And so they came, in great numbers; in the end Méliès was overwhelmed with requests and could not satisfy everyone. Fortunately for the performers, other theatres were open and offered them work.

The Life and Work of One of the World's Earliest Pioneers of Cinema, Georges Méliès, Creator of Film as Spectacle

Andre Deed is a fascinating, generally forgotten, figure in early film history. He was one of the prototypical stars of one-reeler comedies. Between 1901 and 1916, he notched up over 200 film appearances and he directed at least a quarter of these. As his career waned, the two best-remembered film comedians were in the ascendency and both Buster Keaton and Charlie Chaplin would be credited as groundbreaking in that they starred and directed, completely controlling their own work, but they were not the first. His recurrent ridiculous character, Foolshead or Cretinetti, had his own series of films and was popular on a global basis. Deed, along with Max Linder (to whom Chaplin certainly owed a creative debt), very much laid the groundwork for what would become the established fool-in-a-predicament formula slapstick comedies more famously attributed to Mack Sennett. Some of Sennett's early work for Biograph pictures, before he would found his own Keystone Studio, was directly ripping-off Deed's work. By the time Keystone rose to such dominance in the industry a few years later, their prodigious output would render films from other countries unnecessary. Deed's career sank and eventually ended with a job working in the warehouse for Pathe Films.

Some performers from the Comédie Française even ended up working in cinema, but to general amazement, despite their great talent as actors, during the silent era they were found to be inferior, rather like mimes or second-rate artists. Words, their best friend, were denied to them, and being accustomed to the stage their gestures appeared restrained and inexpressive without the script that would have accompanied them, and thus they lost a significant element of their appeal. Naturally enough they were unable to perform in scenes which required sportsmen or performers of great agility. Méliès quickly developed a system of classifying his performers according to their ability, and using them in shoots to which they were best suited; he ultimately assembled a complete and well-trained troupe. But in the special effects scenes he always had to play the lead role, because he could never make his actors understand the infinite details required for the successful realization of a complicated stunt. Only one performer, an acrobat named André Deed who had worked with him for a long time, managed to master a number of the routines set in place by Méliès; he earned for himself a well-deserved success by performing a whole series of burlesque and stunt scenes in Italy, under the name of Cretinetti ('Simpleton').

Another first for Méliès. He was indeed the first person, as far as we know, to use artificial light in a motion picture. Filmed on the stage at the Robert-Houdin, Méliès produced five films from this session known as *Paulus Chantant* or *Comedian Paulus Singing*. The project was Paulus's idea and was the basis of a stunt he concocted in which the film would be shown and, behind the screen, he would be singing live with it in synchronisation to give the effect that the audience were watching a sound film.

To achieve this innovation, Méliès used fifteen arc lamps and fifteen mercury-vapor lamps. Paulus presumably finished the shoot with quite the suntan. Méliès made three of the five films available through the Star Films Catalog. The two he did not distribute were of Paulus (a passionate Boulangist) singing proto-fascist songs, although one must wonder how much influence a film of a proto-fascist song might have had in the silent era. Sadly, all of these films are currently missing.

One final curious detail: it was Méliès who made the first shoots under electric lighting, at a time when this was considered to be impossible, the sensitivity of the negatives being inadequate, as well as the lighting itself. He was nonetheless able, with 30 arc lamps, to film the famous popular singer Paulus on stage in concert. Other cinematographers of the time considered this to be quite extraordinary. Later he would attempt to reproduce this effect in the studio, but there the area to be illuminated was too large, and as incandescent lights did not yet exist he could never achieve a sufficient intensity to work without daylight.

Méliès's testimony is one of the few things to remain from this gathering. No minutes are known to exist and it was seemingly conducted outside the auspices of the media. What is known, retrospectively, is that this meeting, far from the success Méliès claims it to be, was a significant chink in his commercial armour.

Some 200 delegates apparently attended and the day after, a banquet was thrown in the honour of George Eastman, who was present. The most significant of the delegates were invited to remain and a photo was taken to commemorate this. Here is a brief summary of those present at the banquet who, in retrospect, constitute an incredible global assembly of the genuine pioneers of cinema.

FROM THE CONGRESS OF CINEMA TO THE TROUBLES OF AN HONEST MAN

For a moment let us return to the International Congress of 1909. Four nations, the only ones producing films at this time, as we have already seen, were represented. There were around 200 delegates. At the end of the last session many returned directly to their home country, but 50 or so remained and decided to give a banquet on the following day to honour George Eastman who had taken part in the congress and was at this time effectively the sole provider of light-sensitive film in the world. He was already making excellent versions for Kodak before the advent of cinematography. After the banquet a group photograph was taken. We have been able to obtain a copy. We list here the names of those present, many of whom are still well-known: Sciamengo, Gandolfi, Ambrosio, Arribas, Rossi, Ottolenghi, Bolardi, Comerio, May (junior), Jourjon, Helfer, Paul Méliès, Barker, Raleigh, Robert, Reader, de Baulaincourt, Duskes, W. Paul, Hepworth, Cheneau, Effing, Zeiske, Akar, Williamson, Bromhead, Cricks, Brown, Messer, Olsen, Prevost, Bernheim, Vandal, May, Winter, Rogers, Ch. Pathe, Eastmann, Georges Méliès, Gaumont, Urban, Gifford, Smith and Austin. This did not prevent the claims that a Congress which took place much later, after the 1914 war, was the first International Congress. It is our duty as historians to point out this error.

The Life and Work of One of the World's Earliest Pioneers of Cinema, Georges Méliès, Creator of Film as Spectacle

First/front row (from left to right):
George H. Rogers; Charles Pathé; George Eastman; Georges Méliès; Léon Gaumont; Charles Urban; W.S. Gifford; Smith; Austin.

Second row:
Brown; Oskar Messter; Ole Olsen; Alphonse Prévost; Emile Bernheim; *unknown*; Luca Comerio; Marcel Vandal; Charles Raleigh; Ernest May; Winter; Percy Stow.

Third row:
E. Chesneau; Effing; Erich Zeiske; Hubch; Camillo Ottolenghi; Riccardo Bollardi; Akar; James Williamson; Alfred C. Bromhead; George H. Cricks; Alexandre Promio.

Fourth row:
Arribas; Robert Schwobthaler; Ronald Reader; Carlo Rossi; *unknown*; Roger de Baulaincourt; Alfred Duskes; Robert W. Paul; Cecil Hepworth.

Fifth/back row:
Carlo Sciamengo; Alfredo Gandolfi; Paul May; Charles Jourjon; Charles Helfer; Paul Méliès; Arturo Ambrosio; Will G. Barker.

Carlo Sciamengo was the administrative director of Italy's Itala Film. He would also work with Andre Deed.

Alfredo (Alfred) Gandolfi was an Italian cinematographer who made it all the way to Hollywood. His first American film was Cecil B. DeMille's directorial debut *The Squaw Man* (1914).

Arturo Ambrosio was an Italian producer and director who passionately believed in film as an art form and worked hard to create work of a high quality. He directed *The Last Days of Pompeii* (1908) which has been credited as the birth of the Historical Epic genre. His 1924 version of *Quo Vadis* was such a failure that his career never really recovered.

Arribas – I've been unable to find any information on who this might be.

Carlo Rossi was a chemist from Turun who founded Carlo Rossi & C. with investment from industrialist Guglielmo Remmert. Despite initial international success, the company ceased operations within a year and Remmert went on to become one of the founders of Itala Film. Rosi stayed within the industry and became a director at Pathe.

Camillo Ottolenghi ran Turin's Aquila Films, a company initially famed for its focus on telling salacious stories of crime, murder, mystery and violence. They were very successful globally but Ottolenghi was effectively ousted when one of his co-shareholders managed to purchase a larger share and gain more control. Aquila Films was economically crushed by the outbreak of WWI.

Riccardo Bollardi, from Milan, was the president of Milano Films.

Luca Comerio was a photographer who founded Luca Comerio & C. in Milan in 1907. With an initial focus on documentary, the company expanded quickly. Comerio went on to co-found SAFFI-Comerio in 1908, which was an even bigger operation, but lost control of that company the following year when a new major shareholder came aboard, turned the company into Milano Films and jettisoned Comerio who went on to found his own company Comerio Films which lasted right through to 1922, producing over 200 films.

Paul May seems to be representing the French companies Eclipse and Radios. His father Ernest is also in attendance.

Charles Jourjon co-founded Eclair, the French film production company, in 1907. It was credited as the third biggest film company in France after Gaumont and Pathe. Eclair expanded into American and German territories before moving more into technical equipment production in the 1920s.

Charles Helfer was a film agent. He represented the German film company Eiko and Italian film producers Ambrosio Film.

Paul Méliès was Georges's nephew, son of his brother Gaston. Paul followed Gaston into the family business and helped run Star Film in the USA. Later, when Gaston went on his grand journey as a filmmaker, Paul remained in America, running the company and eventually becoming the US distributor for Gaumont.

Will Barker's influence in British cinema can be felt to this day. He entered the industry with his Autoscope Company, screening short documentary films he had shot on a Lumiere camera to a paying public. The success of this and his desire to be able to build film sets led to him building what we now know as Ealing Studios.

Raleigh & Robert (Charles Raleigh and Robert Schwobthaler) were film sales agents based in Paris. They dabbled briefly in film production in France but after a fire destroyed their studio the same year as this congress, their business never fully recovered. A venture to exclusively exhibit the costly and imperfect Kinemacolour system – the first successful colour motion picture process – in Paris was their ultimate undoing.

Ronald Reader was a partner in the American Vitagraph Company, A Brooklyn, NY based studio which pioneered newsreel reporting and expanded to be one of the most significant production companies of the era. Vitagraph was eventually acquired by Warner Bros in 1925.

Roger de Baulaincourt was representing French film production company Le Lion.

Alfred Duskes was one of the pioneers of German silent film. In 1912, with the financial backing of Pathe, he founded the Tempelhof Studios in Berlin, which would become an extremely significant location for German cinema right through the Second World War.

Robert W. Paul has been previously discussed in this book.

Cecil Hepworth was the bedrock of British film production at this time. Having worked for Birt Acres, he went on to become a hugely successful producer, screenwriter and director based in his studio at Walton-on-Thames. He was responsible for creating some of the earliest British film stars, not least Rover, a proto-Lassie screen-dog whose valiant exploits in rescuing children and saving the day inadvertently laid the ground for the visual language of action cinema.

E. Chesneau was the Sales Manager for the Eclipse Film Company in Paris.

Paul Effing represented Deutsche Bioskop. He was an engineer working within cinema and had been inspired by Méliès to work on special effect photography for cinema advertising.

Erich Zeiske was the director of Deutsche Bioskop and a writer/director in his own right. In 1911, he founded the Babelsberg Studios, which exist to this day, in Potsdam, Germany. Murnau's *Nosferatu* and Lang's *Metropolis* were both filmed there.

George H. Rogers was the Co-Founder and Manager of the Eclipse Film Company. He previously had worked for Charles Urban and had crossed Siberia to reach the Far-East to film the Russo-Japanese war of 1904/5.

M. Akar and his partner Emile Bernheim were representing Lux, a French film company. Bernheim was a wealthy Belgian industrialist who had made his money in retail and keenly supported the arts and sciences. He lived to the age of 99, dying in 1985.

James Williamson, from Scotland, moved to Brighton in 1898 with his photographic company. There he made friends with William Friese-Greene and other local photographers who were becoming curious about the moving image. He began producing short trick films which achieved distribution through Charles Urban's Warwick Trading Company. Perhaps his most famous film, *Fire!* (1901) is often credited as creating the basic grammar of film editing in which action can carry on across multiple separate shots when placed sequentially. He went on to form the Williamson Kinematograph Company in London which continued to produce innovative film cameras and equipment right through World War Two, despite Williamson himself dying in 1933.

Alfred Bromhead CBE, along with Reginald, his younger brother, was the founder of Gaumont's British arm. More than a mere foreign distributor, he built British Gaumont up to be a highly reputable production company in its own right.

George Howard Cricks was, at this time, partnered with John Howard Martin in producing films under their Lion's Head Brand trademark. They were vocal advocates for the quality of British film in general, especially their own. Like their contemporaries, they produced a variety of short films – comedies, melodramas and industrial films. In 1911, they moved into feature film production with the fantasy epic *Pirates of 1920*, clearly influenced by the work of Méliès, with its airships and star-filled visual romanticism. Cricks wanted to further pursue the feature-length format but Martin did not. The relationship, and the company, broke down.

By the end of his film career, Cricks was the manager of the film printing department of Gaumont.

The '**Brown**' Méliès refers to could conceivably be Charles Brown of Edison's Kinetoscope laboratory or Theodore Brown, inventor of the Spirograph Projector, but no record exists to confirm this.

Oskar Messter, often referred to as 'the Father of the German Film Industry' was very much born into it. His father founded a company which specialised in optical equipment for the medical and entertainment industries and was a keen proponent of the Magic Lantern shows, creating equipment, including electric lighting for the theatres. Like Méliès, Messter was embroiled in both the mechanical and the theatrical, leaving him in a unique position of readiness for the creation of cinema. Messter manufactured projectors and later moved into film production. He built the Germany's first film studio and continued innovating right through the 1920s, during which he was probably the principal force behind Germany's quest to create synchronised sound for cinema.

Ole Olsen was a film producer and director from Denmark. He was present representing his own company Nordisk Film Kompagni. Nordisk still operates today, over 110 years later, making it the oldest continually-operating film studio in the world.

Alphonse Prevost was a deputy director of Pathe.

Marcel Vandal was a film producer in France, here representing the Eclair film company. He was also an acolyte of the legendary German producer Erich Pommer. Vandal also directed several silent films.

It is unclear who **Winter** might be.

Percy Stow (who Méliès fails to list here but was certainly present) was a very successful British film director from Cecil Hepworth's stable. He struck out on his own and co-founded the Clarendon Film Company in 1904. In all, he directed almost 300 films, including the first cinematic adaptation of *Alice in Wonderland*, which survives to this day.

Charles Pathe, along with his brothers, founded Pathe, a company which exists to this day and was one of the most important forces in the building of the foundations of the global film industry. He is often credited as having been one of the most important figures in the history of French cinema.

George Eastman, the guest of honour, could in many ways be considered the most important person in the creation of cinema. It was Eastman who invented and patented roll film. Up to this point, photography had been achieved using single plates. It was Eastman who pioneered the use of flexible celluloid and the ability to shoot continuous photographic frames. It was this technology which paved the way for the capturing and projecting of the moving image. It made him an extremely wealthy man.

Leon Gaumont remains one of the enduringly mighty figures of French cinema. Initially his company sold stills camera equipment and film but, as cinema emerged, he was at the forefront of production. His secretary Alice Guy was a guiding force in pointing him towards the opportunities presented by narrative film and she went on to become an incredibly successful film director, although until recently, film history has, perhaps misogynistically turned a blind eye to her importance. Gaumont expanded into film equipment production, film distribution and eventually a global network of Gaumont cinemas. Gaumont still operates today and remains one of the most important and successful film companies in the history of cinema.

Charles Urban was a prominent figure in British cinema. An American and an early investor in Edison's technology, Urban would move to London in 1897 and become an agent for Edison films. The following year, he established Warwick Trading Company and went on to set the world standard for producing high quality documentary and news films.

W.S. Gifford was Eastman's Kodak company director in Great Britain.

George Albert Smith would eventually be hailed by Michael Balcon as 'the Father of the British Film Industry' – in many ways he was Méliès's British counterpart and the two enjoyed a friendly correspondence during their heyday. Smith saw the Lumiere's London show in March 1896 and was inspired to embrace this emerging artform. Despite creating and experimenting with innovative optical film effects, he is best known as a progenitor of editing theory. He was at the forefront of establishing the narrative effects of thoughtfully sequencing different shots to tell a more complex and nuanced story. His later career would be dedicated to developing a colour process for cinema. Unfortunately, a patent suit filed against him by William Friese Greene would be his undoing.

The **'Austin'** Méliès refers to might be J. Austin Fynes, a Bostonian Vaudevillian who opened one of Manhattan's first Nickelodeons and went on to promote both live and cinematic entertainment. He would be an early supporter of the Vaudeville child star Buster Keaton.

Throughout his 20 years as a cinematographer Méliès continued to be responsible for the magical productions at the Théâtre Robert-Houdin, and to invent and build numerous visual illusions for it; but as he was at the same time directing his own cinematic productions, his life became hectic and prodigiously active during this long period. Rising at 6am, he was at the studio by 7, building sets, accessories and décor, working ceaselessly until 5pm, in heat which in the summer months could reach 40–45° under the glass panels. Then he would quickly change into more formal dress and leave for Paris where he arrived at his office around 6pm in order to meet those who wished to talk with him. He took a quick dinner, went to the theatre at 8pm, sketched mock-ups during the show, while keeping an eye on the smooth running of the production, left for Montreuil after it was finished and was barely in bed before 12.30, none of which prevented him from rising again at 6 the following morning. Throughout this period of his life he rarely slept more than six hours per night. Fridays and Saturdays were set aside for shooting scenes prepared during the week. These were the most tiring days for Méliès, being at once director, operator and actor. Finally, on Sundays and public holidays, for relaxation, there were matinee sessions from 2–5pm, three regular cinema screenings from 5–7pm, and a theatrical production from 8–11.30pm. Such was his life, without a single day of rest, even on Sunday. He was in fact relentlessly active, thanks to his tireless nature. In August every year he went with his wife and children to the seaside to escape the excessive heat which made life impossible in the studio, all the while preparing new compositions and drawing mock-ups. On the 15th of August he would take the 8am train, arriving in Paris at 11 then in Montreuil at midday, take lunch and then make a shoot from 1–4pm, in order to avoid leaving his public one whole month with no new productions; he caught the return train at 5pm and was back at the seaside by 8 for dinner. This level of activity was typical for Méliès.

As Méliès says, the introduction of film rental hit him hard. His main agenda in the 1909 International Congress had been to convince the most powerful forces in world cinema against the switch to this mode of operation. He had failed. In the early days of cinema, when film production was in its infancy, any entrepreneur with the ability to make film prints available commercially was likely to do a roaring trade in sales. This was a time when small companies maintained the whole process in-house from physically making the films to processing and selling them. By 1909, larger companies like Pathe and Gaumont had become powerhouses and the accelerated rate of production meant there were far more films being produced on a global basis than the demand necessitated. These big companies realised the way to keep their customers onside was to offer them more films at lower prices, so the rental model suited both parties well. The cinemas would no longer have to purchase prints, just rent them for the release period and return them. This placed many of the smaller companies – such as Méliès's Star Films – in an uncomfortable predicament. Their lower level of production and the higher production cost of the better quality films they were offering meant that rental income simply couldn't sustain their business.

The story of Gaston Méliès is a fascinating one and features as a later chapter in this book.

It was for him a period of considerable prosperity. Alas, a whole series of unfortunate events were to suddenly befall him, which would wipe out the great success that he was enjoying. Film rental, which was beginning to find popularity, hit him hard; he was not prepared for working in this way, and as a result the sale of his films was reduced almost to nothing. Nor should we forget that he had no investors and that most of the capital from his profits had been spent on buildings, machines, costume shops, various workshops, and so on – in order to lease, considerable liquid capital is required. He then lost his first wife while his two children were still minors, which caused him great difficulties. Then, without warning, his brother Gaston who ran the New York office had the misconceived idea of wanting to make his own American movies, and to this end travelled across the Wild West with a huge troop of cowboys and redskins. His project was not a success and in one year swallowed up considerable sums, which forced him to close the office and lost Georges Méliès the sums he had invested in it.

Méliès does not directly mention the events which led to the saddest moment in his career. In 1911 he agreed to a deal with Charles Pathe that Pathe would bring Star Films under their umbrella. They would fund and distribute all of Méliès's future films and he would retain a share of any profits made. This deal turned out to be unpalatable to Pathe's shareholders. What resulted was a less favourable arrangement that Pathe himself simply loan Méliès the money to make films in exchange for first refusal on distribution rights and the right to re-edit any films as he saw fit.

This was a bad deal. Artistically and financially. Méliès's films were becoming outdated. Cinema was moving forward and his fantasies in particular were not in keeping with current trends. Méliès took the loan and agreed to put his estate, including his studio, up as collateral.

By 1913, it was all over. His final film *The Conquest of the Pole*, despite being an impressive technical achievement with its massive centrepiece marionette of a Giant, was not enough to save Star Films. The deal with Pathe was over and Méliès lost everything. Including his wife Eugenie who passed away that May.

The outbreak of war was actually unexpectedly beneficial for Méliès. The moratoriums he mentions meant that he got to avoid eviction for a decade. His theatre had been shut down at the onset of war and, when it had reopened, was no longer financially viable. It was eventually demolished. His archive of films met a varied and depressing fate – some had been melted down during the war, others were sold off cheaply to dealers at a bargain price and, as he alludes to, Méliès himself destroyed a significant amount of his original camera negatives in a fire during what might have been a nervous breakdown.

Thus Méliès was already in a difficult position when, out of the blue, the 1914 war broke out. This catastrophe was enough to finish him off. At the beginning of hostilities his theatre was closed by order of police, and his house in Passage de l'Opera deprived of any outlet by the war, he had to resign himself to transforming one of his theatrical studios (the Théâtre des Varieties artistiques, mentioned earlier) and eking out a new existence as a stage actor. During the war he was able, somehow, to survive and look after his family. But in the longer term the overall costs – singers, choristes, actors, taxes, le droit des pauvres (a tax on theatrical productions which contributed towards benefits for the poor), copyrights, etc – were too high, and above all the theatre too small, to recreate the good days. He continued until 1923, but from 1914 to 1923 the rents, insurance, etc, of the various venues which he leased and which yielded nothing, incurred a large number of debts. One moratorium followed another, but eventually the settlement of bills was demanded. At that point, with Méliès financially exhausted and unable to pay, one particular creditor pursued him mercilessly, persuading the Tribunal to order the sale of the property and workshops with no further delay, by legal decree. As happens in such cases, the whole thing was sold at a derisory price, and the loss, for Méliès, amounted to two and a half million. His creditors were uninterested, but he had lost everything and was utterly ruined. It was a devastating blow for him, but one which he bore without flinching.

The Life and Work of One of the World's Earliest Pioneers of Cinema, Georges Méliès, Creator of Film as Spectacle

His pain at leaving his family home, where he had lived for sixty-one years, and in which he had spent his youth among his family, can only be imagined; what a heartbreak when, at the height of his powers, he was forced to abandon the filmmaking that he loved; and what a shock when, over more than a month, junk dealers and scrap merchants took away all the very substantial equipment that had cost him twenty years of hard work and for which, of course, they paid nothing. The same went for the laboratories, shops and facilities of the Passage de l'Opera, and those of Montreuil. The latter included numerous stores, costume shops and a number of sheds, where the most bulky and baroque objects had accumulated, to which only the Chatelet shops could compare: airplanes, balloons, airships, helicopters, trams, cars, rail tracks, locomotives, staircases and scenery, frames of all kinds, furniture from all eras, weapons, accessories of all types – in short, a range of equipment beyond the imagination. Worst of all was that the Lyric Theatre, his last means of existence and situated on his property, was removed as a result of the compulsory seizure of the land, thus taking away his last assets. This collection of bulky material can be attributed mainly to the fact that

Méliès was the first to erect, for his films, gigantic constructions of frames covered with canvas and starch, and decorated to represent rocks, glaciers, caves, hellish or heavenly homes. In these, locomotives, coaches or other vehicles fell victim, on screen, to the most burlesque and fantastic accidents.

In 1923, Méliès, his daughter, his son, his son-in-law and his two granddaughters, the youngest barely four months old, left the family estate for good, without any hope of ever seeing it again. This very large property with a beautiful park, was compulsorily divided up and sold in lots. At the same time, his Paris theatre, the Robert-Houdin, would disappear for the completion of Boulevard Hausmann, and Méliès was with little warning obliged to demand the equipment of this theatre, as well as all that from the Passage de l'Opera, also included in the demolitions. Bad luck continued to hound him. What to do with the boxes containing hundreds of negatives that he had worked so hard to make, since he no longer had any premises at his disposal, and he could no longer continue in his job as a film-maker due to lack of funds? In a moment of anger and exasperation, he ordered the destruction of all this precious material.

The Life and Work of One of the World's Earliest Pioneers of Cinema, Georges Méliès, Creator of Film as Spectacle

It's fairly safe to assume that Méliès knew exactly how rash the destruction of negatives was – it meant that no further positive prints could ever be struck from his vast catalogue of work. An irreversible decision. As an artist he would have been aware of the severity of his action as a strike against his legacy. That said, film was in its infancy and viewed as a consumable and the notion of archiving and preservation was not at the forefront of the minds of even those producing cinema. Recent estimates indicate that between 75% to 90% of silent cinema is lost forever. Luckily, due to his popularity at the time and the continued interest in his work, a significant amount of his work has been, and continues to be, found and preserved sympathetically.

FROM THE DARK DAYS TO THE GALA MÉLIÈS

Clearly he did not think at this time that he was committing an act of irreparable rashness, or he might later have capitalized on the great interest generated by retrospective productions of his work, as witnessed in 1929 at a magnificent gala showing several of his best films which had survived the destruction. They proved to be hugely successful, receiving the admiration of contemporary film-makers.

He had lost everything, but Méliès would not admit defeat; with his family he organized seaside casino concerts during the holiday season, presenting sometimes operettas and at others magic shows, and then when the season was over he continued to tour his productions throughout France. In 1924 he had the good fortune to be invited to Saarbrücken, which at the time was the headquarters of mining company Mines de la Sarre, under the management of French engineers. The association Cercle des Mines asked him to rebuild all the equipment in a large theatre which had been destroyed by the Germans during their retreat. In 5 months, alongside his son André, he rebuilt all the lost machinery and recreated a range of splendid decorations which were acclaimed at their first public presentation.

The woman he married had been his mistress. Jehanne d'Alcy, real name Charlotte Faës, also known as Fanny Manieux, who had been an actress and had known Georges as far back as his purchase of the Theatre Robert-Houdin. She was the star of one of his lesser-known films *After The Ball* (1897). As we know, Méliès did not just make fantasies and science fiction: this film was an exercise in titillation. Credited as one of the earliest stag films, it shows a woman undress to a degree of 'simulated nudity' and be showered by her maid. In the interim years, Jehanne had also married and been widowed. When Méliès wed her, he not only found love but some security too. The shop he claims to have purchased was actually a shop Jehanne already owned and in which he would work.

He returned to France in 1925 and remarried, after 15 years as a widower. His new wife had been one of the first performers at his theatre in 1888; like him she was widowed, and during the war had lost all that she once possessed. Thanks to some money he had put aside, Méliès was able to purchase a small shop for passengers at Gare Montparnasse, a business he would keep until 1932. This was quite possibly the hardest period of his life, since the shop had to be open every day from 7am until 10pm. He could never leave it, even for lunch; no Sundays and no evenings were free. In short it felt like a prison for someone who until then had been accustomed to complete liberty. The shop was in a courtyard and open-fronted, freezing in winter, unbearably hot in summer; a martyrdom for a man already quite old. Alas, he had no choice since he had to make ends meet, no matter what.

Paul Hammond in his book *Marvellous Méliès* describes the Méliès's account of meeting Druhot as apocryphal and offers a different chronology of his rediscovery; that he was first informed by the French Cinematographers' Guild that they would be honouring him, the news of which led to him being asked to contribute a series of articles in Cine-Journal. This publication was edited by Druhot who did, indeed, make mention of Méliès's circumstances to his readership.

There was a very real possibility that Méliès might end his days in these unpleasant conditions, and he worried that illness or injury to himself or his wife could deprive them of this last chance to make a living. However a stroke of luck, purely by chance, brought him some relief. His colleagues from the world of cinema had heard nothing of him since 1914 and believed him to be long dead, because following the disasters that had forced him to leave the business he had become a recluse. Then, one day while passing the Gare Montparnasse, the publisher of Ciné-Journal Léon Druhot heard Méliès name mentioned. He turned to the man whose quite unusual name this appeared to be, and approached him, saying:

'Excuse me sir, I just heard your name mentioned, might you by chance be related to the Georges Méliès who worked in cinema before the war?'

'Why yes,' replied the man, 'Indeed I am his closest possible relative, because I am Georges Méliès himself!' There followed amazement, questions and explanations. Finally Druhot, now in the picture, declared: 'You can't continue to live this way at your age! You are a legend of cinema in France, the world even! Just give me some time – I am going to launch a campaign straight away, and I hope it will bring results.'

In his magazine the following day he published the news of what he had discovered, and launched the promised campaign which was quickly publicized by other industry journals and cinema magazines. It was a revelation. The post-war generation knew nothing of this creator of cinematography, but following the example of the specialist press the daily newspapers took up the story, photographers and reporters laying siege to Méliès at his shop. The articles proliferated, reproduced in regional and then overseas journals. So it was that Méliès came once again to enjoy celebrity status.

Whatever the facts of the matter, undeniably Méliès was being recognised for his contribution and brilliance. The gala was a roaring success. Paul Gilson, one of the organisers, had written a glowing retrospective of Méliès's career in the Revue de Cinema and made a special short film which introduced Méliès to the stage, and back to public acclaim, in style.

Another happy accident came about at this time. Mauclaire, an avant-garde cinema producer, found by chance a dozen of Méliès' great films in an old trunk. They were in colour, but the perforations were of the type no longer used. He got in touch with Méliès and received authorization to make copies and to colourise new prints. Then, with the help of Figaro, L'Ami du Peuple, L'Intransigeant, Paris-Midi, Paris-Soir and other publications, he presented these films as part of a magnificent gala in honor of Méliès, at the Salle Pleyel, attended by the cream of Parisian society and the major players in contemporary cinematography. The theatre was full to overflowing, and people had to be turned away.

The gala was a triumph and, due to the high price of tickets, made a good profit. That evening would be one of the high points of Méliès' life; his films, so different from those we see today, provoked wild enthusiasm and rapturous applause.

As for those who worked in the cinema industry, they were stunned that 30 years previously, with the most rudimentary equipment, it had been possible to make films so perfect, complex, technically accomplished, and delightfully hand-coloured. It is certain, moreover, that the mechanical methods used nowadays for the colouring of films, using (whatever the method) a limited range of colours, could not come close to the infinite variety of tones achieved by true artistes using the full chromatic scale; the evidence was right before their eyes. The audience left the gala both charmed and thrilled. Mme Thuillier, the colourist who had worked on Méliès' films with the help of some 200 assistants, came from her rural retreat to witness this event and was deeply moved to rediscover, after 20 years, the man she had believed to be long deceased. She too received well-deserved applause.

The Life and Work of One of the World's Earliest Pioneers of Cinema, Georges Méliès, Creator of Film as Spectacle

The result of this gala – which would be followed by many others in a number of theatres including Mauclaire's Studio 28 – was a flurry of articles praising Méliès. The Chambre Syndicale Française de la Cinématographie (the French Cinematographers' Guild) was impressed and its president, Louis Aubert, gave a speech at its annual banquet which caused a sensation. Before the 800 industry figures present, he concluded his speech with this declaration: 'We, the elders, know; but you younger people are unaware that it is to Méliès that we owe the success of the cinemas which we operate today, and that those among us who have made their fortune also owe it all to him. Regrettably, cruel setbacks and undeserved misfortune brought him down; it is only fair that we do the right thing by him, and that he should regain his rightful place in our industry.'

These words were acclaimed by those in attendance, and Méliès was the object of a prolonged standing ovation. Shortly afterwards Méliès was granted a retirement pension which, while certainly modest, freed him from the worry and weariness which he had known for the previous six years.

The Life and Work of One of the World's Earliest Pioneers of Cinema, Georges Méliès, Creator of Film as Spectacle

The Mutuelle du Cinema's retirement home had been established in 1921 in Orly, a suburb of Paris. Méliès gives the impression that he is now at peace with himself but this was not an easy period for him. Although his accomodation was financially covered, Méliès and Jehanne were without personal finances. Even covering the train fare to Paris, less than 8 miles away, proved difficult. During this time, Méliès was a prolific writer of letters. The world of cinema had progressed exponentially and new groups – cineastes, film journalists and film historians – had many questions for him. His correspondence kept him busy and there was even an ongoing possibility of a return to work for him; for a while, he was attached to a collaboration between Marcel Carne and the Prevert brothers in which he would serve as Technical Advisor on the film *The Phantom of the Metro* but this eventually floundered. Perhaps most tantalising was the opportunity that he might work with Dadaist film-maker Hans Richter on a new version of *Baron Munchausen* but, ultimately, this was also not to be.

AT THE HOUSE OF THE MUTUELLE DU CINEMA

The 'Mutuelle du Cinéma' owns a superb estate at Orly, near Paris, with a chateau and a park, which was to become the retirement home of the 'cinématographiques'; it is in one wing of the chateau that Méliès lives today with his wife and one of his granddaughters, aged 13 (who was just 4 months old when he left Montreuil). She is the daughter of Méliès' daughter, now deceased. Her father Fontaine, known in the theatre as Fix, has continued to work as a singer and is almost constantly on tour. This is why Méliès, as a conscientious grandfather, has taken responsibility for this particularly intelligent girl's education — she came first in a competition in which all the schools of the Seine département took part. She is now his pride and joy, but this does not prevent him from always taking an interest in developments in the world of cinema. He is frequently consulted for information on the history of cinema, and his memory, as with all his mental faculties, remains faultless. It is indeed quite surprising that his past misfortunes have in no way changed his natural good nature. The only event which he will never get over is the death of his daughter, who was his devoted collaborator and whom he adored. Having helped her father in his cinematic work as an energetic young girl she married Fontaine Fix, and on becoming an opera singer she adopted the name of Madame Méliès-Fix. In 1914 she worked as a volunteer nurse in a military hospital, became known for her limitless devotion to the wounded, and at the end of hostilities she received a number of decorations. While working diligently in this role throughout the four war years, she and Méliès put on numerous plays and fêtes for her hospital and gave her all, despite the demands of her job. She was a superb performer as well as a woman of good heart. Sadly, during a tour in Algeria, she contracted a serious illness which would finally end her days after two years of terrible suffering.

The Life and Work of One of the World's Earliest Pioneers of Cinema, Georges Méliès, Creator of Film as Spectacle

Georges's son Andre would live to the age of 84, dying in Paris in 1985. He worked sporadically as a film actor, his final role being in the film *Thomas the Imposter*, written by Jean Cocteau. His most memorable screen role, however, came in 1952 when he played his father – alongside his mother as herself – in the biopic *Le Grand Méliès*.

Georges Méliès' son André is himself in almost constant demand as a leading man in operetta, usually far from Paris, which he only visits once or twice a year. This too is a matter of great regret for Méliès, not having close to hand the son who was for a long time his partner and collaborator in the variety theatre at Montreuil. As we so often see, a consequence of war has been the regrettable separation of a once close-knit family.

To this day, films by Méliès which have been long-considered lost continue to surface in the most unlikely places. The 2017 documentary *Saving Brinton* shows the films *The Triple-headed Lady* (1901) and *The Wonderful Rose Tree* (1904) both being discovered in the basement of an Iowa farmhouse and subsequently delivered to Serge Bromberg of Lobster Films, who have done incredible work restoring and exhibiting the Méliès archive for a modern audience.

Bromberg himself, being interviewed for this book, was bleak about the outlook going forward. Around 230 films have been discovered in the last century and time is running out for the around-300 which remain missing. Early film is decaying fast, without professional preservation and restoration whatever remains of Méliès's work out there is rotting in the cans and might be beyond saving when eventually uncovered.

It will be remembered that duplicate negatives of Georges Méliès' films existed in his New York office. When the office closed these negatives were placed in storage with the original American manufacturer of animated-film projectors, an American of French heritage named Le Roy. Then, during the war, they were stolen from the Le Roy's basement by a burglar, who was looking for something else altogether. The burglar sold them to an American who, having paid for them, had the audacity to feature them in commercial retrospective revues, while refusing all authors' rights to Méliès. However these films were protected by copyright and Méliès sought to deny their exhibition, unless he were offered some form of legitimate indemnity, either in the form of payment or a positive print of the most significant films. This proposition came to nothing but the purchaser, being unable to profit from his acquisitions, finished by offering (or maybe selling) the negatives to the Museum of Historic Motion Pictures in Los Angeles. They remain there today, as Méliès learned from the American ambassador at the banquet recently held in honour of Louis Lumières by the Society of Motion Picture Engineers at the Hôtel Crillon in Paris. So, late in the day, luck would have it that not all Méliès' extraordinary work was lost for good.

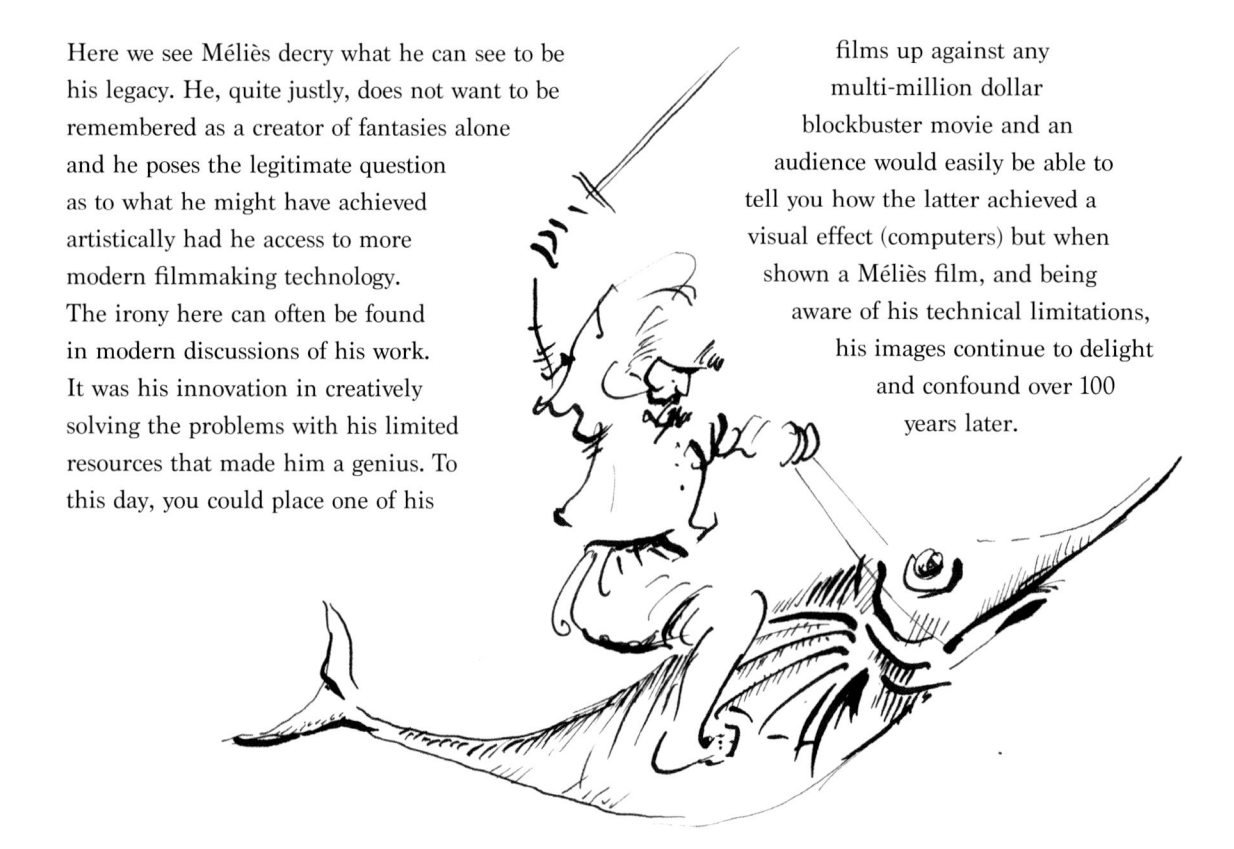

The Life and Work of One of the World's Earliest Pioneers of Cinema, Georges Méliès, Creator of Film as Spectacle

Here we see Méliès decry what he can see to be his legacy. He, quite justly, does not want to be remembered as a creator of fantasies alone and he poses the legitimate question as to what he might have achieved artistically had he access to more modern filmmaking technology. The irony here can often be found in modern discussions of his work. It was his innovation in creatively solving the problems with his limited resources that made him a genius. To this day, you could place one of his films up against any multi-million dollar blockbuster movie and an audience would easily be able to tell you how the latter achieved a visual effect (computers) but when shown a Méliès film, and being aware of his technical limitations, his images continue to delight and confound over 100 years later.

We must now conclude this appraisal of Méliès' contribution to the cinematographic art. Contrary to received opinion, Méliès did not only produce works of magic or fantasmagoria, but covered all genres. However the undeniable mastery, the limitless imagination and the continual inventiveness that he brought to his compositions ensured that it was their popularity with the public which compelled him to produce a great number of such films; their originality created his reputation as a 'brazen illusionist'. The truth is that his artistic talent allowed him to produce work in all styles. One need only look through his film catalogue to see that his 'fantasmagorical' films represent not much more than one third of his huge total output. Unfortunately, Méliès was ahead of his time. What might he have produced with the resources available to today's film-makers? None of this, neither apparatus nor lighting, existed at the time.

Although, perhaps lacking in modesty, what Méliès says here is not untrue. It could be said that the reason his work resonates so strongly still and transcends the perfunctory inelegance of early cinema is that he was artistically far too sophisticated for cinema at that time. When Méliès made his name, cinema was a sideshow gimmick. To see movement in an image was worth the price of admission alone and the notion of a cinema, as a building built for and dedicated solely to film projection, was in its infancy. The middle class had yet to embrace the medium. It certainly was not considered art for some time and the audiences must have frustrated him deeply.

The progress of modern times is due above all to electricians and set builders; beyond that, the actual composition of scenes has barely evolved. It is well known that, for a long time, educated people were reluctant to attend cinema screenings. Equally it is known that Méliès was a designer and painter, in a word an artist, and consequently could never be satisfied with the shabby experience that was early cinema. But we must also recognize that even if Méliès attempted, right from the beginning, to present cinema as an artistic medium and was at the time misunderstood, the fault lies to a much greater extent with the public than with him. It was a long time before he was in a position to create works which required a certain cultural awareness on the part of the audience for their true worth to be appreciated. What can one do for people who, accustomed to crude buffoonery, would consider a Méliès film 'idiotic' purely because it was beyond their understanding?

Much of Méliès's documentary work is missing and unlikely to be found. Lacking what we would characterise as his thematic hallmarks, his artistic style, film credits, the Star Films logo, or even an appearance from the man himself, his documentaries might well still exist in archives all over the world but there is no way of specifically identifying them.

This is why, abandoning the historical, mythological or educational themes which he had attempted to popularize, Méliès decided to make films in the fantastical and comedic genre, and at this moment he struck gold. This new style allowed limitless possibilities for his imagination, made possible the most comical scenes, and at the same time enabled him to achieve effects previously thought impossible. He had therefore found a medium which satisfied an uncultured audience but also intrigued the curious and was appreciated by those of a more artistic bent. This style of composition allowed him to embark on works of pure invention or dream sequences, and to create beautiful, fantastical, fairy-tale scenes. Furthermore, he had the great advantage that this type of spectacle could be immediately appreciated by a wide public, without any need for explanation.

Méliès strength was that he was never deterred by any difficulty; once he had decided to create an effect, nothing could stop him. He was, in short, a great inventor with the gift of enormous energy and perseverance. He was also an innovator in the most diverse genres, as if he were aware of what cinematography would go on to achieve. It might even be said that he also understood how cinema could play a role in education or instruction. When he started there was no question of cinema being considered an educational tool, yet he attempted to make films with the intention of giving children, and even adults, what were then called leçons des choses (general science lessons). Thus, from the first year, we find in his films a laundry, a smithy, a perfume factory, a pottery workshop, a cotton mill, the unloading of a boat on the quay at Le Havre, the Marseille docks, farm work and a fire being extinguished, among others.

Urban had tried his best to get a film camera into Westminster Abbey but come up short so filmed documentary footage of the outside events of Coronation Day and hired Méliès to reconstruct the interior ceremony, to be cut in.

Méliès worked from photographs sent by Urban and pulled off a convincing job – even with a King Edward VII performed by a local washhouse attendant.

These documentaries were made at a time when street photography was censured by the authorities and no one would dream of sending out film reporters, who would come up against the same restrictions; this happened to Mesguisch, Lumière's first operator in the US. Méliès solved this problem by recreating sensational events in his studio, not without some difficulty. Thus he produced The Eruption of Mount Pelée in Martinique; the Shipwreck of the battleship Maine in the port of Havana and the visit to the wreck by divers; and later, the famous Dreyfus Affair, and even the Coronation of King Edward VII in Westminster Cathedral (re-enacted in his garden in Montreuil). In *Les Incendiaires (Histoire d'un Crime)*, a complicated and significant drama, he even reconstructed the execution of a man condemned to death. All this appeared so natural and was achieved with such skill that the audience believed they were seeing the real thing.

However these documentaries were of little interest to the public of the time, who preferred to be entertained, and quite apart from this some of the films caused Méliès a degree of trouble. For example, at screenings of *L'Affaire Dreyfus*, over-excited supporters and enemies of Dreyfus fought in the theatre, provoking the police to intervene and ban the film in France. In *Les Incendiaires* the final guillotine scene was so realistic that women fainted, leading to this scene being cut by the censor; the film closed with the condemned man waking in his cell, the blurred vision of the sinister device in the distance.

These various problems meant that Méliès stopped working in these genres, which he found less enjoyable and which were nowhere near as profitable as his fantastical works – it is for these reasons that he increased production of the latter. When, at the request of M. Urban, head of the Warwick Trading Company and Méliès' agent in London, he recreated the coronation of King Edward VII – a major undertaking expertly carried out – something extraordinary happened: a Parisian newspaper accused him of being a faker! Everyone in London knew that entry to the cathedral was strictly forbidden to photographers and filmmakers, and in its advertising campaign Warwick had made it known that it was spending fabulous sums of money to recreate the coronation scenes inside the cathedral, without which film of the celebrations outside would be sadly lacking.

The Life and Work of One of the World's Earliest Pioneers of Cinema, Georges Méliès, Creator of Film as Spectacle

Public interest was undiminished and the film, screened in the Alhambra and Empire theatres, in all the great music halls of England, and before the Court itself in Windsor at the request of the king, was a great triumph. The king even told Urban, 'if I did not know that the king and the queen in the film were only our doppelgangers, I would be convinced that were watching ourselves, so perfect is the resemblance'. In fact, the king having undergone an operation shortly before his coronation, the traditional ceremony had been somewhat shortened to avoid causing him too much fatigue, but Urban had insisted that the filmed ceremony be absolutely complete. The result was that the king, after the screening, said to Urban: 'My congratulations, it is splendid! What a wonderful invention cinema is! He found a way to record even those parts of the ceremony that did not happen! It's really fantastic!' And everyone laughed, of course.

Méliès, too, had great fun with the Parisian journalist's accusation and replied to him, with the greatest seriousness in the world: 'When I screened, some time ago, the life and death of Joan of Arc, battles from the Middle Ages and Antiquity, the story of Julius Cesar, Olympus, Jupiter, the Muses and the mythological divinities, be sure my dear sir that no one thought for a moment that I was trying to deceive the public into believing that I had filmed all this in past centuries… The Coronation of the King was presented as a "reconstruction", so let me advise you that the word "faker" seems to me, to be polite, at the very least exaggerated and certainly extremely naïve…'

There is truth to Méliès's self-penned epitaph here. Not only was he a technical innovator, an inventor of special effects which are still routinely used to this day, not only did he bring fantasy and magic to cinema, not only did he create cinematic science fiction but he also was in the advance guard of professional production, studio filming and global distribution. Other than him, it's hard to name another person in cinema history who neared this 'purity' which he defines – someone able to finance, produce, write, direct, set-build, star in and sell a film. The Auteur Theory was some years away from conception, yet here is a man with total control of his cinematic output.

George Méliès became seriously ill with cancer late in 1937. On January 21st 1938 he died in Paris, in the Hopital Leopold-Bellan and was buried four days later in the Pere Lachaise Cemetery.

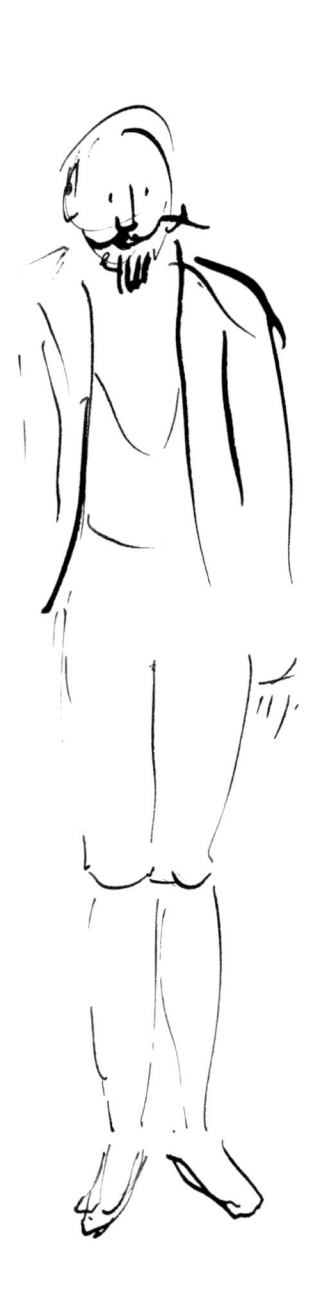

Finally, we present the titles of Méliès' most significant works, those which, for 20 years, were screened the world over. It would be impossible for us to name them all, for he was a tireless producer and inexhaustibly creative. As Andre R. Mauge wrote in *La Revue des Vivants* (October 1931): 'When one sees Georges Méliès' work in cinema, it is astonishing that such long films could be made with such primitive inventions, works which were a dizzying concoction of comical finds and hasty improvisations. But there you have it! Georges Méliès made his films alone, taking orders from no one. Nowadays, the best directors achieve relative independence only after a long struggle. Méliès did what he wanted; that is why his work retains, despite the years, such marvelous innocence, a purity that was set free and will not be found again. He simply expressed, through the means at his disposal, what his genius dictated to him."

THE END.

Translation of *Cinematic Views*

A 1907 article by Méliès

As fascinating and important as Méliès's autobiography document is, I must admit that when I discovered the following article, I was far more taken with it. Méliès wrote the following piece for *Annuaire Général et International de la Photographie* – an annual publication of essays by people at all levels and disciplines of the photographic industry which gave a snapshot of current developments, concerns and practices. In the 1907 edition, Méliès describes, with great depth and attention to detail, the exhausting process of realising a commercial film. This piece is rich with technical specificity and is, even now, a perfect primer for anybody interested in understanding the film-making process in the early 20th century. Of particular interest is the section in which he elucidates the issues surrounding actors struggling to adapt to a new form of performance and the role of the director in aiding them with this. He even touches upon film budgeting and the necessary application of intelligence to production design.

This is a far more focused and coherent statement. Gone is the frustrating third-person voice and insecurity of the previous document. Here we find Georges as expert and educator who gives us insight, not into his life or art, but into his craft.

CINEMATOGRAPHIC VIEWS

BY GEORGES MÉLIÈS.

My intention in this address to the reader is to explain as best I can the thousand and one difficulties which industry professionals must overcome in order to produce work which is of artistic value, entertaining, bizarre or even naturalistic, and which at this moment is in great demand the world over.

The most experienced industry professionals, of which I am one, would require numerous volumes to record all that they have learned from day to day during their long years of continuous practice, and the space at my disposal is unfortunately very limited. So my intention here is to present the largely unknown aspects of film-making and in particular those difficulties which the public might never imagine, encountered at every stage in the production of works which ultimately appear quite simple and straightforward.

On numerous occasions at screenings I have heard the most improbable comments, which prove without any doubt that a substantial number of the spectators could not begin to imagine the amount of work involved in the films they had been watching. Some, understanding nothing of how 'it it comes into being', simply and naïvely conclude 'it's trickery!', or 'they must do it like that in the theatres!' And, satisfied with their explanation, they end with 'it is well done all the same!'

Obviously, anyone who thought about it for one minute would not express such an opinion: the lack of daylight in the theatres, the impossibility of properly illuminating the stage and sets in a regular and reliable manner with magnesium lamps, theatrical mimicry (as we will see later), and the very limited length of film reels are all factors that make it almost or completely impossible to shoot film in these conditions. The painting of stage sets, itself, has a distorting and destructive effect in cinematography, as I will explain in the section on decoration. Some make no attempt to understand this, and care very little.

Yet there exists a category of viewers who, by contrast, would not be at all unhappy to receive some information in order to satisfy their curiosity. This is absolutely legitimate and natural among intelligent people who wish to make sense of what they are seeing. It is these people, certainly greater in number, whom I hope will appreciate this lecture.

Let's start with a few words about cinematographic equipment.

The Cinematograph [moving picture camera]: Today everyone understands the principle of the cinematograph, so it is not necessary to describe it in detail. Suffice to say that it is made to photograph objects or people in movement, by capturing the various stages of movement in a series of successive images captured at very short intervals, on a film which turns behind the lens. Generally these images are shot at a speed of 12, 16 or 18 per second as appropriate for the speed of movement of the object being photographed. The device is operated by a hand crank, turned with greater or less speed in order to obtain more or fewer images per second. When filming objects which are almost immobile a slow speed is sufficient. By contrast, when objects, people or animals move across the scene at great speed it is necessary to turn the crank faster and obtain more images, to avoid the streaking and blurring which would otherwise inevitably appear on each photograph. If the object is close to the device the crank must be turned even faster. This is all a question of practice. The light-sensitive film, which is contained in a hermetically sealed box on top of the device, is turned by means of a special mechanism and passes behind a rectangular window at the back of the device. It does not move continually but rather in successive jolts, stopping and recommencing between 12 and 18 times per second, according to the speed at which the crank is turned. With each stop, the film is moved up and down 2 centimetres; and as soon as it stops a shutter automatically opens to allow the photograph to be exposed on the film. This shutter is then immediately closed until the next stop. This produces a series of photographs 2 centimetres high and 2.5 centimetres wide, from one end to the other of a roll of film which, as soon as it is exposed, is fed into a second box, also hermetically sealed to daylight. If we look at the images obtained after development we will see that any gesture, for instance that of a person raising their arm, is represented by five or six different images in which the arm in question will each time move higher; the movement is deconstructed and reproduced in successive stages. If the film was moving continuously without stopping, and without the shutter interrupting its movement, we would see a blur where the arm has moved instead of a series of clear images. As for the stopping and restarting of the film, this function is achieved, according to the device in use, either by a cam, by a Maltese cross, or by cogs moving vertically and horizontally, which grip and pull the film by its regular perforations which run along the edges of the film from one end to the other. There is no need to enter into detail concerning the mechanisms of the various devices in use. Whatever system is used to move and stop the film, the principle is the same: to take, at very close and regular intervals, a specific number of successive photographs of the moving object.

I will not go into any technical description of the cinematograph itself, because there are already countless works giving all the necessary information, and my intention is to discuss not the Cinematograph, but cinematographic films.

The different types of cinematographic films: There are four main categories of cinematographic film; or at least all films can be considered to belong to one of these categories. There are so-called outdoor films, scientific films, compositions, and so-called transformations. I intentionally define these classifications in the order in which cinematographic films have followed one another since their first screenings. The first films were exclusively of subjects taken from nature; later, the cinematograph was used as a scientific device, then eventually becoming a theatrical device. From the beginning, its success was enormous, due largely to curiosity at the appearance of animated photography; but when the cinematograph was put at the service of theatrical art, success turned into triumph. Since then, the popularity of the marvelous instrument has only increased, on a phenomenal scale.

Outdoor films: Those involved in cinematography all started out working in the open air; and all of them, whatever the speciality to which they have devoted themselves, have continued on occasion to do so. These films reproduce scenes of everyday life in cinematographic form: films shot in the streets, in public places, at sea, on river banks, in boats, on railways; panoramic views, ceremonies, parades, processions, etc. It is, in short, the replacement of documentary photography, once made with portable photographic cameras, by animated documentary photography. The film-makers — having at first shot very simple subjects which caused amazement purely through the novelty of movement in photography which had hitherto been frozen in immobility — today travel all over the world to bring us the most fascinating scenes. We now see, with minimal effort on our part, countries which we would probably never have visited, with their costumes, their animals, their streets, their population, their manners; all this presented with a fidelity which can only be described as…

photographic. The landscapes of India, Canada, Algeria, China, Russia; waterfalls, snow-covered countries and their sports; foggy or sunny regions; everything has been filmed, to feast the eyes of those who are happy not to go too far out of their way. The film-makers who have specialized in this branch are numerous, for the simple reason that it is the easiest. Having an excellent instrument, being a good photographer, knowing how to select your vantage points, not being afraid to travel and to move heaven and earth to obtain the necessary authorizations, are the only qualities required in this field. Undoubtedly this is not inconsiderable, but we will see later that all this is just the art in infancy. Any film-maker can shoot nature films, but not everyone can compose scenes.

Scientific films: Soon after the appearance of animated photography, people had the idea of using the cinematograph to capture anatomical studies of movement in humans and animals on film. M. Marey, who before the invention of the cinematograph proper succeeded in filming — by deconstructing movement using a photographic camera with several successively triggered lenses — a flying bird and a galloping horse, was the first to achieve this extraordinary result. Today, thanks to the cinematograph, the automatic camera par excellence, this is a possibility available to everyone. Others have added a microscope to the cinematograph, and have given us fascinating views of the actions of infinitely small creatures and organisms; others have used the cinematograph to record and reproduce, for a selected audience of students, surgical operations performed by a master, or to screen general science, glasswork, the working of steam or electric engines, pottery, and industries of all kinds. With the possible exception of microscopic studies which require special equipment and knowledge, this special branch of cinematography could, if need be, fall under the category of so-called outdoor films, since as in the former the operator here limits himself to recording what is happening in front of him. But all things considered it was felt necessary to accord this special branch of cinematography its own category.

Compositions: We now come to staged compositions of various genres. In this category fall all productions, whatever they be, where the action is prepared as in the theatre and performed by actors in front of the machinery. The variety of this kind of film is endless, from sketches, comic opera and burlesque to the most serious drama, via comedies, folk plays, courtroom dramas, clowning, acrobatics; graceful, artistic or eccentric dance; ballets, operas, plays, religious lessons, pornography, les poses plastiques (living statuary), war scenes, news; reproductions of the various events, accidents, catastrophes; crimes, assaults, etc, and who knows what else? Here, the scope of the cinematograph is boundless, any subject imaginable is fair game and is seized upon. It is in particular this and the following branch that have immortalised the cinematograph, because like the imagination the subjects are both infinitely varied and inexhaustible.

Transformations: I finally reach the fourth category of cinematographic films. The exhibitors called this 'transformational films', but I find the name inappropriate. Since I have created this particular branch myself I will be allowed, I think, to state here my opinion that the name 'fantastical films' would be much more suitable. This is because, if a certain number of these films indeed involve changes, metamorphoses, transformations, there are also a large number where there is no transformation; rather there are many elements such as theatrical props, staging, optical illusions, and a whole series of processes which as a whole can only be described as 'trickery', a name that is not very academic but has no equivalent in the chosen language. Be that as it may, the scope of this category is by far the most extensive, since it encompasses everything from outdoor films (not prepared or falsified, though taken from nature) to the most significant theatrical compositions, encompassing all the illusions that conjuring, optics, photographic rigging, theatrical decoration and props, lighting, and dissolving effects (as the English call them fadeouts) can produce, as well as a range of whimsical fantasy compositions wide enough to drive the most intrepid researcher mad. Without any intention of belittling the first two categories, I will now deal exclusively with the last two, for the very simple reason that I will be entirely in my element and that I will be able, therefore, to discuss it in full knowledge of the facts. Since the day, going back ten years, when innumerable film-makers threw themselves into shooting outdoor films and good, bad or indifferent comic sketches, I stopped working in this area and created the specialism of creating films which are interesting due to their difficulty of execution, and to which I have since exclusively devoted myself. This is what earned me, moreover, a visit from Mr. Roger Aubry, who asked me to explain, for the readers of this yearbook, the genesis and the process of artistic cinematographic films. I do it with a pleasure all the greater since I passionately love this extremely interesting art to which I have entirely devoted myself; it offers such a wide variety of research, requires so much work of all forms, and so much attention, that in all sincerity I have no hesitation in proclaiming it the most attractive and interesting of all the arts, precisely because it uses almost all of them: drama, illustration, painting, sculpture, architecture, mechanics, manual work of all kinds, everything is employed in equal measure in this extraordinary profession; and the astonishment on the part of those who, by chance, have been able to witness some part of our work in progress always brings me the greatest enjoyment and pleasure.

The same phrase invariably returns to their lips: 'This is quite extraordinary! I could never have imagined that it would take so much space, so much equipment, and that it required so much work to make these films! I had no idea how it was done.' Alas, they are not much wiser afterwards; one has to spend a long time getting one's hands dirty, so to speak, to know completely the innumerable difficulties to be overcome in a profession which involves creating everything, even what appears impossible, and to give the appearance of reality to the most chimerical dreams, the most improbable inventions of the imagination. Finally, it goes without saying that one must indeed achieve the impossible, since it is photographed and is thus seen!

For our particular branch of work we had to create an ad hoc workshop. Simply put, it is a combination of the photographic workshop (on a huge scale) with the theatre stage. It is constructed from coated iron; at one end are the units housing the equipment and the camera operator, while at the other end is a floor built exactly like that of a theatre stage, featuring hatches, trap doors and skylights. Of course, on either side of the stage are wings, with decor stores, and behind, dressing rooms for the performers and extras. There is a below-stage area with sets of traps and cushions necessary for the sudden appearance or disappearance of evil spirits in fairy tales; annexes where props are packed away during scene changes, and above them a grille concealing the wheels and winches necessary for the manoeuvring of heavy objects (flying characters or chariots, angels, fairies or swimmers, etc). Special pulleys are used to move panoramic canvases; electric searchlights illuminate sudden apparitions. It is in short, on a small scale, a fairly faithful reproduction of fantasy theatre. The stage is about ten metres wide, plus three metres of wings in the courtyard and garden. The total length, from stage front to the filming apparatus, is seventeen metres. Outside, there are iron sheds for the construction of wooden props, scenery, etc, and a series of workshops for building materials, accessories and costumes.

Daylight and artificial light: The ceiling of the workshop is partially glazed with frosted glass, and partly with ordinary glass. In summer, when the sun shines on the scenery through the windows, the effect could be disastrous, as the shadows of the roof joists would stand out distinctly on the canvases below. Therefore a set of movable shutters, activated by wires which can open or close them in a split second, is employed to resolve this problem. The frames of these shutters are lined with tracing canvas (such as that used by architects to draw their plans) which, when closed, allows a dim light, similar to that of frosted glasses. Consistency of light is very difficult to obtain during the performance of a shoot which can sometimes take four consecutive hours or more to produce a scene which, when screened, might be between two and four minutes long. Then, in cloudy weather, those wretched black clouds seem to enjoy constantly obscuring the photographer's friend the sun, producing an inevitable sense of exasperation for the person directing the camera operators, scene shifters, machinery operators, actors and extras. It requires the patience of a saint; sometimes we wait for the clouds to clear, sometimes we close the shutters if there is too much light or reopen them if there is not enough, all without losing sight of the thousand details of the work in progress. If I'm not mad now I probably never will be, because hazy, cloudy or foggy skies have tested my patience to the limit… and throughout my career have caused me to write off countless shoots, incurring huge expenses. Any scene interrupted or abandoned due to bad weather, while frustrating for the actors, can double, triple or quadruple its cost, depending on whether we need two, three or four days in a row to complete the shoot. I have known scenes take eight consecutive days, including the two-and-a-half-minute Faust ballet which cost 3,200 francs. It was enough to drive anyone mad.

So, after much trial and error, and despite the whole thing often being declared impossible I very recently managed to create — by means of a special electrical installation composed of battens, pulleys and struts similar to that in theatres —artificial lighting which reproduces perfectly the effect of daylight, and which will finally free me from the hard labour necessary in the past. God be praised! I will not go crazy, at least not because of clouds… The diffuse light is achieved using an appropriate combination of a very large number of arc lamps and mercury vapor tubes. This artificial light is used concurrently with daylight, and varies in intensity as required.

Composition and preparation of scenes: The composition of a scene, a play, drama, fairy-tale, comedy or artistic tableau naturally requires the creation of a scenario drawn from imagination; then the search for effects that will impress the audience; the drawing of sketches and building of models for sets and costumes; the establishment of the main story, without which no film has any chance of success. When dealing with illusion or fantasy, the invention, the combination, the sketches of the effects and the preliminary study of their construction require special care. The staging is also prepared in advance, as is the positioning of extras and the placement of stage-hands. This work is absolutely analogous to the preparation of a play in the theatre, with the difference that the author himself must combine everything on paper, being therefore author, director, draftsman and often actor, if he wants to create an effective piece of work. The creator of the scene must direct it himself, because success is absolutely impossible if ten different people get involved. Above all, we must know what and who we want, and insist on the roles they will play. We must keep in mind the fact that we will not rehearse for three months as in a theatre, but for a quarter of an hour at most. If you lose time, the day is wasted… and you can forget filming. Everything must be planned, even and especially the pitfalls to be avoided – and in the special effect scenes, there are many.

The decor: The sets are assembled following the approved mock-up; they are built in wood and canvas in a studio adjoining the installation workshop, and painted with distemper, like theatrical decoration; except in this case the painting is exclusively done in grisaille, passing through the whole range of gray between pure black and pure white. This makes them look like funeral decorations and appears very strange to anyone seeing them for the first time. Décor in colour will go horribly wrong: blue becomes white; reds, yellows and green become black. The effect is completely destroyed. It is therefore necessary that the sets be painted as if they were photographic backdrops. Painting is done with great care, contrary to that of theatrical scenery. The finish, the exact perspective, the skillfully executed trompe-l'oeil giving the impression of real objects in panorama, all this is necessary to create the appearance of reality in entirely fake constructions which the camera will photograph with absolute precision. Anything that is badly done will be mercilessly exposed in the shooting; therefore, one must stay focussed and do everything with meticulous care. All this I know. When it comes to scenery, the cinematographer must aim higher than the theatre director, and not accept the conventional.

The props: The props are made of wood, canvas, cardboard, paste, moulded cardboard, moulded earth; or are borrowed everyday objects. However, if we want to achieve a good photographic result it is best only to use – even for chairs, fireplaces, tables, rugs, furniture, candelabra, clocks, etc – specially made objects, painted in various shades of gray, carefully shaded, according to the nature of the object. Since high-end cinematographic film is often coloured by hand before screening, it would be impossible to colour real photographed objects, which, if they are in bronze, mahogany, red, yellow or green fabrics, would become an intense black and therefore lack all transparency; as such it would be impossible to recreate the true translucent tone necessary for screening. This is an aspect that the audience is generally unaware of, and they certainly have little idea of the time and care that goes into the making of props that appear simply to be natural objects.

The costumes: For the same reason, most costumes must be specially made in tonalities that reproduce well when photographed and may later be hand coloured. Hence the director's need to have at his disposal an enormous store of costumes of all kinds, of all ages, of all nationalities, and of all conditions, along with their accessories – this is without listing the array of hats, wigs, weapons, jewellery – from the great lords to the lowliest hoodlums; the costume shop, however large, is still not enough. With ten thousand repertory costumes in use, it is not uncommon to occasionally hire from theatrical costumiers to complete platoons when many similar costumes are needed – mainly in parades or processions using a great number of extras. Naturally, costume-makers as well as repair and maintenance staff are necessary; the same goes for underwear and swimwear, as well as for shoes and other equipment.

Actors and extras: Contrary to popular belief, it is very difficult to find actors who adapt well to the cinematograph. Many excellent theatre actors, even star performers, are absolutely worthless in a cinematographic shoot. Often even professional mimes are bad, because they perform according to conventional principles, just as ballet mimes have a particular style that is immediately recognizable. These artistes, undoubtedly superior in their specialism, are lost as soon as they are in front of the cinematograph. This is due to the fact that cinematic mimicry requires specific training and qualities. There is no longer an audience for the actor to address, either verbally or by mime. The only spectator is the camera, and there is nothing worse than to watch and direct an actor performing for the first time, not to a theatre audience but to the cinematograph. The actor has to accept that he must make himself understood, while remaining mute, to the 'deaf' who are watching him. His performance must be serious yet very expressive; little gestures, but very clear and very precise. Performances of perfect facial expression and correct physical posture are essential. I have seen many scenes played by renowned actors; they were not successful precisely because the main element of their success, the word, was absent in front of the cinematograph. They will say that they use gesture only as an accessory to speech in the theatre, whereas in cinematography speech is nothing, gesture is everything. A few, however, have been successful in this medium, among them Galipaux. Why is this? Because he is accustomed to using monomime (solo mime artistry) in his monologues, and has the gift of a most expressive physiognomy. He knows how to make himself understood without speaking, and his gestures, even deliberately outrageous ones, which are necessary in mime and especially in filmed mime, are always of the greatest accuracy. An actor's precise gestures, when used to accompany his word, are no longer at all understandable when he mimes. If you say 'I'm thirsty' at the theatre, you will not hold out your thumb with your hand clasped to simulate a bottle – it's completely pointless, since everyone has heard that you are thirsty. But in mime you obviously have to make this gesture.

So it's very simple, is it not?

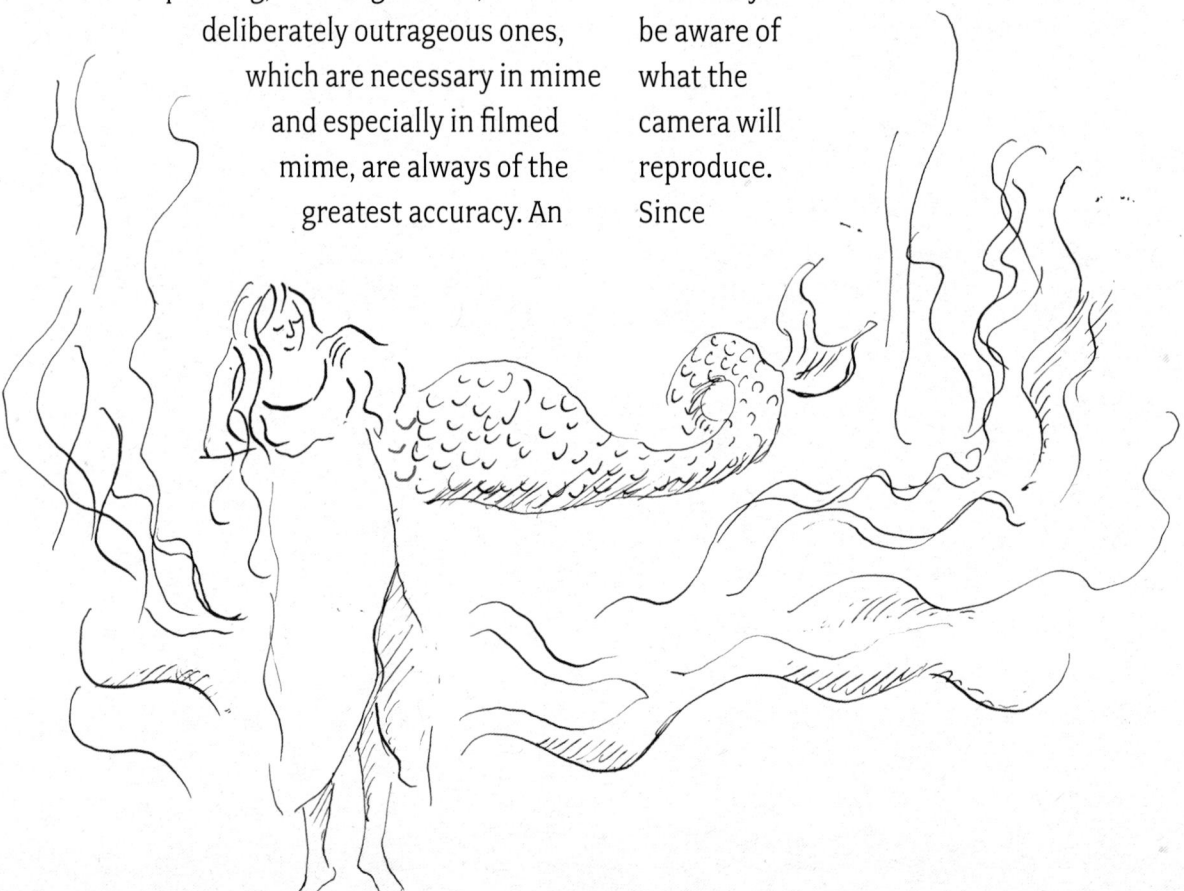

Yet, nine times out of ten, it will not come easily to anyone who is not practiced in mime. Nothing is improvised, everything is learned. It is also necessary to be aware of what the camera will reproduce. Since the characters appear together in a photograph, alongside one another, we must take great care always to highlight the main characters, and downplay the performance of the secondary characters, who are often prone to making inappropriate gestures. When filmed this produces a mish-mash of mingling people; the audience no longer knows who to watch and we have no understanding of the scenario taking place. The phases must be sequential, and not simultaneous. Hence the need for the actors to remain disciplined, and to perform only in turn, at the precise moment when their intervention becomes necessary. There is one more thing that I often had difficulty in making artists understand, as they always sought to make themselves noticed to the detriment of the scene and the work as a whole: generally, they are over-keen. And how carefully one must tread to rein in this keenness without crushing it! Strange as it may seem, each one of the artists employed in my quite extensive troupe was chosen from some twenty or thirty that I auditioned in turn without identifying the necessary qualities, although all were very good artists in their respective Paris theatres.

Not all of them have the necessary qualities, and unfortunately keenness does not replace these qualities. Those who have ability adapt quickly; others, never. Among women artistes in particular, those who succeed are rare. Many are attractive, intelligent, beautiful women, and wear the costume well; but when it is necessary to make them mime a scene it becomes somewhat difficult, alas! Three times alas! Anyone who has not witnessed the work that the director puts in cannot begin to understand. I hasten to add that, thankfully, there are an exceptional few who perform very well and very intelligently. In conclusion: assembling a good cinematographic troupe is a long and difficult process. Only those who have no concern for art would be happy with the first performers they find who manage to botch together a confusing and uninteresting scene.

Costs: The costs occasioned by the cinematographic shoots are very variable and depend essentially on the work to be produced. Cinematographic film today costs about 0.5 francs per metre for the negatives, and the same for the positives. It follows that, as raw material, a strip of 20 metres is 10 francs for the negative and 10 francs for the positive, or 20 francs for the lot, if you shoot just one test. This is nothing, of course. If it is a question of shooting a scene in India, in America or elsewhere, it is mainly the traveling expenses which considerably increase the cost of the finished project. In the case of compositions, the value of the 20 metres can vary to infinity, depending on the work involved in the shoot. Some will shoot scenes using four or five characters played by second-rate artistes and performed in rudimentary fashion in the street, in a garden, on a road, on a farm, etc. In this case, the costs will be minimal. Others, on the other hand, will employ numerous staff including highly-remunerated artistes, and use expensive sets, props and costumes; in such a case, the expenses are considerable. As a point of information, a great historical or fantasy piece, an opera, can have between thirty and forty scenes, requiring two-and-a-half to three months of preparation, twenty to thirty sessions, with a staff of twenty to thirty artistes, one hundred and fifty to two hundred extras, twenty machinery operators, dancers, male and female dressers, hairdressers, costume makers, etc. Sometimes painting scenery, especially for special effects, has to be repeated several times over before it is perfected. In short, the completed production will entail expenses of all kinds amounting to 12,000, 15,000, even 18, or 20,000 francs, for a total of 400 metres of film, which gives a screening of twenty-two to twenty- three minutes' duration. The viewer who pays 0.5 or 1 franc for his seat has no idea of these significant details. This is also the reason why the price of printed cinematographic film is by necessity so widely varied, depending on the producers and their kind of work. It is also generally not known that the fees paid to top performers are so great that most of them earn more per month from the companies that employ them for cinematographic work than in the theatres to which they are attached. This is an excellent new outlet for performers, to whom the filmmaker has brought a serious windfall and a much appreciated salary supplement.

Special effects: It is impossible in this already long talk to explain in detail the execution of the cinematographic special effects. That would require a presentation of its own, and even then only practical experience could bring a detailed understanding of the processes used, which pose extraordinary problems. I can – without boasting, since all it is recognized by everyone in the industry – state here that it is I myself who successively discovered all the so-called 'mysterious' processes of the Cinematograph. All the editors of compositions have more or less followed the path which I established, and one of them, the head of the largest film house in the world (from the point of view of large-scale low-budget production), told me: 'It is thanks to you that cinema has been able to sustain itself and become an unprecedented success. By applying animated photography to theatre – that is to say to infinitely variable presentations – you have prevented it from the failure that would soon have been the fate of outdoor productions, which are formulaic and of which the audience would soon have tired. I confess, quite shamelessly, that if there is a triumph, it is this triumph above all that makes me happiest.'

   Do you want to know where my idea to apply this approach to the Cinematograph originated? It was quite simple, actually. A fault in the device I used early on (a rudimentary device, in which the film tore or often stuck and would not advance) produced an unexpected effect, one day when I was making a routine film at the Place de l'Opéra: It took a minute to release the film and restart the camera. During this moment passers-by, buses and carriages, had of course moved. When viewing the film, at the point where the fault occurred, I suddenly saw a Madeleine-Bastille bus transformed into a hearse and men changed into women. I thus discovered the substitution trick known as stopwatch, and two days later I performed the first metamorphoses from men into women, and the first sudden disappearances that were to be so successful in the early days. It was thanks to this very simple effect that I presented the first fairy tales: Le Manoir au Diable, Le Diable au Couvent, Cinderella, etc. One thing leads to another, and following the success of this new genre I attempted to develop new effects. I imagined, sequentially, changes of decor achieved by fadeout through using a particular function of the camera; appearances, disappearances or metamorphoses obtained by superposition on black backgrounds, or specific black areas in the sets; then superimpositions on prepared white backgrounds (which all declared impossible until they witnessed them) which are obtained by way of a trick which I am not at liberty to discuss, my imitators having not yet discovered the secret. Then came the effects of severed heads, of double exposure of scenes played by a single character who, by double exposure , ends up playing up to ten similar characters in one scene. Finally, employing my particular knowledge of illusion that comes from twenty-five years of practice at the Théâtre Robert-Houdin, I brought tricks using machinery, mechanics, optics, conjuring, etc to cinematography. When these processes are combined and used skilfully, I have no hesitation in saying that in cinematography today it is quite possible to achieve the most impossible and the most improbable effects.

   I will conclude by admitting that, to my great regret, the simplest effects are the ones that have the most effect, and that those obtained by superimpositions, many of the most difficult, are appreciated only by those who understand the difficulty involved. Among others, the scenes played by a single character in which the film is exposed sequentially up to ten consecutive times in the camera in order to record, are of such difficulty that it comes to resemble a Chinese puzzle. The actor, playing ten different roles, must remember at every second, while the film is turning, what he did at the exact same moment during the previous takes, and the exact place where he was on the stage. On the one hand this is the only way that the performance of ten artistes (who are in fact one) can exactly match; on the other hand, if in one of the takes the actor makes a misplaced gesture, for example where his arm passes in front of a character photographed in the previous take, it creates double-exposures and blurring that spoil the effect. One can thus understand the level of difficulty, and the rage that consumes you when, after three or four hours of hard work and attention, a break in the reel at the seventh or eighth take forces you to to abandon the film under way and redo everything; it is not possible to sequence a torn reel for further takes, and where the image is still latent it can only be developed once the tenth and last superposition has been recorded.

   This may be 'Hebrew' to those unfamiliar with the process, but I can only repeat that detailed explanations would take too long. In any case, it is the intelligently applied effect which today makes it possible to render visible the supernatural, the imaginary, even the impossible, and to achieve scenes of true artistry which are an absolute delight for those understand how all the fields of art contribute to their execution.

Difficulties and drawbacks: As well the obstacles already mentioned, that is to say the difficulties inherent in the performance of these kinds of scenes, there are others that can frustrate the cinematographer: these are variations of light, clouds passing across the sun, mechanical problems with the camera, the reel sticking, the film tearing, lack of sensitivity of the emulsion, the spots or dots which appear on certain films after development and make them unusable, the specks which are invisible to the naked eye but appear large as rocks when screened. So we experience great relief when we are able to declare, after development, that the shot is perfect. No one, among the uninitiated, can know how much patience, perseverance and determination is necessary to achieve success, and I can not help but smile when I hear people say, 'how come these films cost so much?' I myself know only too well; but how to spell it out to someone who has no idea how this work is done and who is looking for just one thing in a film: cheapness!

Shooting and the camera operator: It goes without saying that the operator for this particular genre must be very experienced and very familiar with many tricks of the trade. The execution of a difficult shoot cannot be undertaken by a beginner. He will invariably miss the most cleverly executed tricks if, while turning the crank, he forgets the slightest detail. An error in turning, a missed number counting aloud while shooting, a micro-second of distraction means all is lost. It takes someone calm, attentive, thoughtful, able to cope with annoyance and irritation. And indeed, annoyance and nervousness are almost inevitable when one is faced with innumerable difficulties and unpleasant surprises that are almost continual. These few observations will explain why the shooting of fantastical films – depending equally on the director, the machinery operators, the actors and the camera operator who makes the shoot – is so difficult. It is the perfect harmony, the attention of all, the close co-operation which is so hard to obtain, while at the same time we grapple with practical difficulties of all kinds.

This will be enough to explain why, having at first enthusiastically embraced this new genre, most film-makers have given up on it. You have to be more than a simple camera operator for this kind of production and, if the cinematographers are numerous, those who have succeeded in doing something outstanding are very few: still barely one per nation, since all the countries of the world depend on French manufacturers for artistic films.

Rehearsals and execution: A word now on the actual execution of the piece. When a set is complete and the decor finished with along with the props, accessories and, if they are required, the effects, the costumes for the scene are prepared in their dressing rooms for the performers who convene for the following day. As in the theatre, they arrive punctually, which is essential since the sun will not wait. After a concise explanation of the character they have to play, their costumes are given out; they dress, apply makeup, in short prepare their character as they would in the theatre. But here again, they do not escape the law that governs the painting of sets, in which only white and black are used. Thus, no more rouge on the cheeks nor on the lips, unless they want to resemble negroes. Makeup is done exclusively in white and black. It is a particular art which requires some learning, because there is a discipline to be observed in order to present characters who are clearly identifiable but not ridiculous.

The artists, as directed by the stage manager, enter the stage. There, the producer, who is usually also the director, first explains the scene to be played in its entirety, then orders brief run-throughs of the various stages of the performance; the main scene first, then the other scenes. He directs the movement, the positioning of the extras, and must enact the role of each of his characters to indicate their gestures, their entrances, their exits, the position they must take on stage. He pays great attention to separating his groups so that the presentation is not confusing, and that the viewer always follows the continuity of the main scene even when certain characters are off-stage. All this requires a great familiarity with the process, a concise and absolute precision in the explanations, and the cooperation of intelligent performers and extras, who must understand straight away what is asked of them.

We must never forget that the pitiless sun rises and sets, and that if all is not in position, primed and ready to photograph at the right moment, the best time of day will pass and it will be necessary to postpone, thus doubling the expense. All being well, we move on to the dress rehearsal; if something goes wrong, we put it right and start again. Finally everything is ready. The actors play the scene and speak as they would in theatre, which creates a more realistic performance. The camera operator sets his device in motion and everything that happens is recorded. If we are to shoot a second scene, the scenery is changed as soon as the first is over, the performers dash off to the dressing rooms to change costumes, and everyone comes back on stage.

The same work of direction, explanation and rehearsal starts again, and the second scene is performed and filmed. I always keep in mind that we must work fast while forgetting nothing because, except in summer, favourable daylight hours are short and one must not lose a second. A complicated scene sometimes requires two or three days of consecutive takes. It is not uncommon to take eight or nine hours shooting a scene which will last two minutes at the screening; this occurs particularly in scenes with transformations and superimpositions, hence their great cost.

Development and printing: I stated at the beginning, that I did not intend to go into great technical detail from the filmmaker's point of view; this goes back to the basic principles of photography. Suffice to say, for the uninitiated, that the printed film is developed in one of two ways, according to the production house: either on frames, around which the film is rolled, with gelatin on the outside; or on drums or cylinders, on which it is placed in a spiral, in the same way. In the first instance, the frames are slid into grooved developer tanks, where they stay as long as is necessary for development. The overseer removes them from time to time and examines everything in transparency, as he would with ordinary plates. If film is developed on drums, it is placed in semi-cylindrical tanks, inside which they turn on their axis. The rotation is achieved either by hand crank, similar to the cylinders used for roasting coffee, or by an electric motor, which allows a single overseer to monitor the simultaneous development of several drums.

Washing and fixing are done by transporting frames or rolls from one vat to another, containing water and hyposulfite Finally, the last wash is done, by plunging them into the running water as with ordinary plates, and, for the drums, by rapidly rotating them in the constantly renewed water. Rotational washing is much faster, which is advantageous for mass production. Finally, the films are spread out on very large cylinders of 1.5m diameter which are turned electrically at a great speed. In about an hour the films are dry.

As for the production of the test prints, it is done by passing a sensitive virgin film applied, gelatin against gelatin, on a single frame. The two films pass together through a device identical to that used to make the shot, but the lens is replaced by a square window in front of which is placed an artificial light. The light prints the image exactly as it prints positives on glass projection plates.

    Cinematography has become a colossal industry, today employing more than 80,000 people throughout the world. Hard to believe, yet it is the truth, and its success is only increasing from day to day. Why is this? Because, the world over, such an intriguing presentation is an irresistible attraction; and this being the case, the cinematographer is able to present superb performances at a very affordable price in countries deprived of theatre or other such distractions, since the impresario, once he has bought of the film, does not have to pay fees to the artist.

    Ah! If only this were the case for theatre directors! But there it is, nothing can compare to the filmed artistes who perform calmly and faultlessly in cinematographic shoots. They can never be inconsistent, good one day and bad the next; if they perform well at first, they are excellent in perpetuity. What an advantage!!!

The Other Méliès

The name Méliès has echoed through cinema history but is rarely prefixed by the name Gaston. For, as great as Georges' achievements indisputably were, he was not the only member of the clan who directed films and it could even be argued that his older brother Gaston's story is a far, far, more exciting one…

Centre Point is one of London's modern-age landmarks. Built in 1963, it was one of the United Kingdom's first skyscrapers and a key example of the era's Brutalist movement in architecture. It remains, by far, the tallest building in its area and sits somewhat incongruously, even now, with the smaller historical buildings that surround it on London's famous Tottenham Court Road. A hundred years earlier, on that exact spot stood a building called Imperial Mansions, which housed offices. One of which was, from 1890, the rather unhappy base for the failing footwear sales company of Georges' brothers, Gaston and Henri. They had stayed in the family business after having bought Georges out. It wasn't going well. In 1893, their fortunes seemed to be looking up as they secured a big military contract for the supply of boots but within two years it was all over, thanks to the price of leather rising and the contract being cancelled.

Within a decade, Gaston would be a vital part of the new family business. Whatever shoes he had left were about to take a pounding as he headed out into the world. As cinema was born, so was its nemesis – piracy. Particularly outside France, Georges was struggling to exert the copyright he held over his own work. Edison was the king of all pirates, but by no means the only one – the Lubin company in particular bootlegged Méliès's work mercilessly. Edison's executives had realised that producing their own films was needlessly expensive when the costs of 'duping' European imports in their labs were negligible. They even squeezed extra profits by selling on the original prints they had used to dupe. Méliès's name was not used in conjunction with the illegal release of his films and Edison even had the cheek to sell hand-coloured versions at an inflated price. The amount of money Méliès was losing from the American market alone was staggering and his response was bold.

In 1902, Georges put Gaston on a boat to New York where he would aggressively represent the copyright of Star Films. His official words on the matter, upon establishing their premises on East 23rd Street, were "In opening a factory and office in New York we are prepared and determined energetically to pursue all counterfitters and pirates. We will not speak twice, we will act!"

157

Georges began shooting his films with a double camera set-up for the purposes of creating two original negatives. One stayed in Paris with him, the other was sent to Gaston in New York where the films were copyrighted by sending complete paper prints of the negative reel to the Library of Congress in Washington.

As a side note, this method of producing two negatives has, only recently, led to a rather spectacular and wonderful result of which Méliès himself would have doubtless been overwhelmed with excitement. It turned out that the distance Méliès placed his two cameras apart (as close as he could, to get as similar result in each negative as possible) was almost exactly the same distance as required by the two lenses in modern 3D filmmaking. This means that the combination of the two angles can produce a full 3D effect. In 2010, Méliès' modern champion Serge Bromberg presented a simulation of this effect to great acclaim at the Cinémathèque Française, using sections of Méliès films of which both versions exist.

Star Film were now their own distributor in the U.S. and reaped the benefits of that. Méliès also installed agents representing the company in various territories around the world. Within a year, Gaston's son Paul was working alongside him and Star Film's American operation was strong enough for them to dip their toe into the notion of production.

Back in the U.S., Edison had shrewdly, greedily, hoovered up the patents on pretty much anything related to the production and exhibition of the moving image at this time and he protected them fiercely. Filmmakers knew his Motion Pictures Patents Company as 'The Trust'. It was a body dedicated to controlling or crippling Edison's competitors and he used federal law enforcement officers as his heavies. The Méliès brothers were not impervious to this and had signed up to become a part of the M.P.P.C. Georges and Gaston both held licences with Edison which allowed them to export their negatives from France to the U.S. to produce positive prints for distribution. The M.P.P.C, however, cancelled this arrangement when they considered a business deal Gaston had made with American entrepreneur J.J. Lodge had led to a breach of contract. The legal dealings surrounding this are, perhaps, what lead to Gaston forming the Méliès Manufacturing Company and consequently producing his own films.

Gaston had previously produced four tentative films himself in the U.S. Spread out over four years, all were documentary. His first appears to have been footage of the 1903 America's Cup yacht race in the New York City Harbour in which the New York Yacht Club's Reliance beat the Royal Ulster Yacht Club's Shamrock III. Gaston's focus at this time, however, was business. He returned to Paris in 1907 and, within a few months, was on his way back to the U.S. with a new bride, Hortense Louise, in tow.

In 1909, something changed. Perhaps emboldened by his dismissal from the M.P.P.C, Gaston, although still charged with duties to his brother Georges, became a filmmaker, starting out as producer on *The Stolen Wireless* – a short drama of romance and revenge set against a backdrop of war, starring Francis Ford, whose younger brother John would go on to become a legendary director.

Shortly after, Gaston took the reins himself and directed Francis in *For The Cause of Suffrage*. Working regularly with Ford, Gaston began to make a string of non-documentary shorts for Star Films, often directing himself, sometimes overseeing William F. Haddock in the director's chair.

At this time in cinema, the most essential ingredient to any film was not story, star or genre, it was light. The notion of a studio as a place to film was in its infancy and even the ones which existed would be unrecognisable to the modern industry. Electric light was not yet the norm so these studios were not cavernous, soundproofed dark spaces as we now recognise them; they were glass structures designed to bring in as much light as possible.

Most films, quite simply, were shot outside. Even films set inside. If you look very carefully at a lot of early silent films, you'll notice a strong breeze and maybe even a hint of rain blowing through many a living room or bedroom. Being located on the East Coast of the U.S. meant that Gaston's new enterprise was becoming a seasonal affair. Once summer had passed, the limited hours of daylight and the poor weather made outdoor filming impractical. Gaston despatched Paul and film director Wallace McCutcheon south to Texas to investigate the potential for filming there.

What they discovered was not just a location but a genre. Although it's acknowledged that the first ever Western film was 1903's *The Great Train Robbery*, the Western as a genre really didn't explode until 1910, the year Star Films arrived in San Antonio, where they quickly became part of the zeitgeist.

The Star Films Ranch comprised a two-storey farmhouse and a decent-sized barn situated on a patch of land of around 20 acres, leased from The Hot Sulphur Wells Hotel. This was useful as the hotel also provided luxurious accomodation for the more important members of the Star Films company. A place suitable for actors of repute. Gaston swiftly joined them and a schedule of work to rival Georges's in Montreuil began.

Although all but a precious few films remain today, the Star Film Ranch was a production powerhouse. Between 1910 and 1912, they made around 140 one-reel movies, mostly Westerns with the occasional comedy. Usually a Western comedy. Like his brother, Gaston was not immune to the attraction of the occasional performance in front of the camera where his favoured role was that of a priest.

His regular cast still featured Francis Ford but the true star of the enterprise was Edith Storey. Storey had proven herself a talented screen actor in some Vitagraph pictures but, under contract to Star Films, her incredible talent as a horse rider made her a star. Films were built entirely around her ability and she fast became the doyenne of the Western chase film.

Along with his stable of regular actors, Gaston keenly used real local cowboys as the cast in his pictures. This enthusiasm for authenticity and slight blurring of the lines between fiction and documentary would become a deeply significant hallmark of his work as it progressed.

The most significant film Gaston produced during this period was his 1911 epic *The Immortal Alamo*. This was the first film ever made concerning the 1836 Battle of the Alamo, one of America's most significant and recounted skirmishes. Francis Ford and Edith Storey starred. Sadly, this film is now lost and no copies are known to survive but documentation from the time asserts that Gaston negotiated that director Haddock be granted access to shoot some of the film at the historical site of the Alamo itself. It is also documented that a Cattleman's Convention in town that week brought tens of thousands of visitors into the area, making filming somewhat problematic. At just ten minutes long and with a plot which focused on an apparently fictional romance, the recreation of the battle itself was somewhat compromised and the film drew mixed reviews.

That same year, Gaston moved the family studio out to the Sulphur Mountain Springs resort in California to be closer to the new centre of West Coast filmmaking. In an impressively short amount of time, cinema as an industry relocated from the East Coast to California. It happened for largely the same reason that Gaston had migrated to the U.S. in the first place – Edison. The iron fist of the M.P.P.C had led to the smaller studios and distributors moving en masse to the West Coast where they knew Edison would have a harder time keeping tabs on them and that they were close enough to the Mexican border to make a run for it were he to come after them. The location had the added benefits of year-round sunshine, beautiful locations and a union-free workforce who expected far lower wages than their east-coast counterparts. This mass migration to California and the establishment of various studios in proximity would within a few years formalise and coalesce into what we now know as Hollywood.

Gaston however, despite being one of the founding pioneers, would never become a part of Hollywood. In an newspaper piece titled "Tired of Cowboys", Gaston tells the press that, bored with producing Westerns, he is taking "a complete cinematograph outfit consisting of operators, stage managers, and a complete dramatic company" on a voyage to the South Seas "for the purpose of gathering fresh material in novel settings for moving pictures". And that is precisely what he did; in all, a team of 22 including his wife Hortense, star of *The Immortal Alamo* Fanny Midgley, and screenwriter Edmund Mitchell.

The story of Gaston Méliès is really that of his grand voyage. The term 'South Seas', now slightly dated, referred to what we recognise as Asia-Pacific which was, at that time, largely unspoiled by Western capitalism. On his tour, Gaston filmed almost constantly and produced over 60 films between 1912 and 1913. This adventure was full of largely-forgotten cinematic firsts. In some places he was the first to shoot moving pictures at all, in others the first to produce fiction films and, quite significantly, he was one of the first filmmakers in history to actively collaborate with indigenous populations and cast them to play roles in his films. The norm at this time was to paint the face of white actors to inhabit any ethnic roles and often those roles were no more simple than that of a savage. Gaston did not entirely escape this stereotype. His portrayal of indigenous cultures was often as comic relief to the white leads and he is reported to have complained of the locals he encountered as being "not savage enough". But he did cast local talent and was also keen to tell local stories. He was enthusiastic about capturing these exotic cultures in as authentic a way as possible to share their beauty with the rest of the world.

Sailing from San Francisco on 24th June 1912, the ocean liner The Manuka carried Gaston and his crew to their first port of call. Tahiti. He was already in production as they left port. Onboard the liner, he began to roll camera on his first "Around The World" film, an equator-crossing comedy called *The Misfortunes of Mr and Mrs Mott on Their Trip to Tahiti*. It's a comedy of errors which goes on, after some hilarious misfortunes aboard The Manuka, to present audiences with some of the first ever filmed images of Tahiti. The capital city Papeete is presented in tantalising documentary shots before we are reminded that our focus might also be the Motts.

Onboard The Manuka, Gaston had, by chance, befriended the governor of Tahiti which led to extraordinary access once they disembarked. Amongst the rare and culturally relevant footage he would shoot would be a cinematic glimpse of Tahiti's queen. Indeed, Gaston was moving in high Tahitian circles; having met the queen he would go on to be the houseguest of her brother. Gaston made a total of 9 films in Tahiti, spanning documentary, comedy and romance. The Governor lent him his yacht and Gaston made a brief trip to Bora Bora and rolled camera on footage of the fishermen there.

From Tahiti, Gaston sailed to New Zealand, landing in Wellington. By this point, he had fallen out with some of his crew – most notably

Bracken who was drinking too much and did not share his boss's work ethic – so some of them were sent back to the U.S. Gaston met and befriended writer James Cowan in Wellington. Cowan had grown up in an area with a large Maori community and, after a stint as a journalist for the New Zealand Herald, moved his career toward the documentation of Maori culture. He spoke the language fluently and led Gaston into this world. Although Gaston produced travelogue documentaries throughout the country, his interest lay in the world that Cowan opened up for him. They travelled to Rotorua where, finding a troupe of Maori performers, Gaston hired Cowan to write screenplays for him to feature an entirely native cast.

Gaston produced and directed a film of *Hinemoa*, a local legend and in so doing created what is believed to be the first fiction film made in the whole country. He and his new cast followed this up with *Loved By a Maori Chieftess* and *How Chief Te Ponga Won His Bride*. He also shot a short documentary piece – *The River Wanganui*.

On to Australia. Gaston, Hortense and what remains of their crew arrived in Sydney but found little inspiration and headed instead for Melbourne, via Brisbane. From his base here, Gaston headed to Barambah, a reserve where he met the local Aboriginal people. Keen, once again, to make films featuring a native cast, he completed a couple of action pictures replete with spear-throwing and boomerang attacks. Cowan was an expert with a boomerang and gladly assisted with these scenes. The team moved on to Gympie and produced some fictions about gold prospectors before reaching Cairns to work with the Aboriginal people there too. Disappointed to not find the natives as tattooed as he had expected, Gaston instructed that fake tattoos were applied to the cast. This playing-up of the stereotypes has led him to be criticized in recent years.

Gaston's next port of call was Java. Here, he travelled to Borobudur to film the temple and the dancers there. From there, via Batavia to Singapore where, again, he filmed what are believed to be the first fiction films in that area. Continuing with his travelogues, he also assembled a documentary called *A Day at Singapore*.

From Singapore to Cambodia where he filmed the ruins of Angkor-Thom – one of the few films of his which survives to this day - and a couple of romantic and comedic fiction films. Gaston filmed a lot more documentary footage around the capital Phnom Penh too, where he was embraced by the King and awarded a medal. The oppressive climate and various illnesses had now begun to plague what Gaston named 'The Wandering Star Film Company'. The travel and conditions on this voyage were often difficult and several members had succumbed to this. From Cambodia, Gaston wrote to his son Paul admitting that even he was feeling the exhaustion.

The SS Atlantic took what remained of the team to Japan and, upon arrival, Gaston sent a few of them straight back to America. Fanny Midgley, who had accompanied him on the entire trip and been very ill for the more recent legs, was given her leave to return with them. She resumed her career back in America and even shared the screen with Valentino, although no longer as the female lead.

Despite intense bureaucracy from the Japanese authorities, Gaston assembled a small, amateur troupe of local actors and a director and built a temporary studio space in Yokohama to film in. Concentrating on fiction films, as both Vitagraph and Pathe had already cornered the market in documentary footage of Japan, Gaston again made the effort to tell indigenous stories. The only surviving piece of footage from Gaston's time in Japan has turned out to be a significant one. He gained permission from Kanō Jigorō, founder of the Kodakan and creator of Judo, to film within the Kodokan for the first time ever. With two cameras, Méliès filmed a Judo display and captured some of the fathers of the discipline demonstrating their techniques. This remains some of the earliest and most important martial arts footage.

In May 1913, Gaston realised that his adventure had come to an end. His son Paul, back in the U.S., had struggled to make a success of the films that he received and money was running out. Gaston, now seventy years old, called it a day. Only five of his original crew were still with him and he sent them home. Gaston and Hortense returned to France and eventually settled in Corsica.

The financial loss was devastating. Vitagraph took over the U.S. arm of Star Films and Paul Méliès became a U.S. distributor for Gaumont. Georges blamed the voyage and his brother's spending for the entire collapse of Star Films - they never spoke again.

Gaston's voyage had been a bold and ambitious undertaking. He filmed people and places which had previously never been captured by a movie camera. He immersed himself in local indigenous cultures and brought their stories and legends to life. He endeavoured to send postcards back to the Western World of truly exotic cultures and, perhaps regrettably, embellished these when he found them not quite exotic enough. Gaston, like (although also very un-like) his brother Georges was a cinematic pioneer, yet his name is largely forgotten.

The tragedy of Gaston and the body of work from his grand adventure is that so very little of it survives. Of the estimated 64 films that he made in these countries, almost nothing survives at all. The majority of the film negatives that he shipped back to Paul in New York had been ravaged by the atmospheric conditions and technical impossibilities of the trip, so this footage was unusable and therefore represented a great financial loss. The films which did make it to market were not well received, tastes had moved on - even Georges was experiencing this. Of the commercial prints which were distributed, very few survive and there has yet to be a significant conservation and restoration effort made that might commemorate Gaston.

If it weren't for the dedicated hard work and research of film-maker and writer Raphaël Millet, who has been incredibly generous in sharing his work with me for this chapter, the story and achievements of Gaston Méliès would be a mere footnote to his brother's legacy.

Gaston Méliès died on April 9th 1915 due to shellfish poisoning. He is interred in Hortense's family tomb in Montmartre, Paris. ★

Georges Méliès Filmography

This is as complete a list of Méliès films as currently exists. It's taken from the very well-maintained George Méliès Filmography Wikipedia page and is always the most up-to-date public resource as to which of the films are currently known to exist. The list is chronological as to production and is based mainly on the official Star Films catalogues. It uses their numbering method too, so although it might look at first as if there is more than a thousand films extra to what you have been led to believe, it is actually based on reels. In the earliest days of film, a reel would last about a minute and measure around 65 feet in length. As film narratives got longer, Méliès would sell two-or three reelers and by 1912 he was producing films which could reach 13 reels in length.

The films after 1911 were released by Pathé, so don't have numbers.

The bulk of this filmography is the work of Jacques Malthête from the 2008 book *L'Oeuvre de Georges Méliès* but it includes work from filmographies compiled by Paul Hammond and John Frazer.

Each entry notes whether the film is lost, survives or a fragment remains.

Many of the surviving films are available to watch on YouTube but the quality both of the original prints and the digital files varies wildly. The best way to view the surviving work of Méliès is through the DVD and Blu-ray collections available on the Lobster Films and Flicker Alley labels.

1896

1. *Playing Cards*
   Une partie de cartes **Survives**
2. *Conjuring*
   Séance de prestidigitation **Survives**
3. *Smarter Than the Teacher (1st bicycle lesson)*
   Plus fort que le maître (leçon de bicyclette) **Lost**
4. *Gardener Burning Weeds*
   Jardinier brûlant des herbes **Lost**
5. *A Merry-go-Round*
   Les Chevaux de bois **Lost**
6. *Watering the Flowers (comical subject)*
   L'Arroseur **Lost**
7. *The Washerwomen*
   Les Blanchisseuses **Lost**
8. *Arrival of a Train at Vincennes Station*
   Arrivée d'un train (gare de Vincennes) **Unknown**
9. *The Rag-Picker, or a Good Joke*
   Une bonne farce (le chiffonnier) **Lost**
10. *Place de l'Opéra, 1st view (Paris)*
    Place de l'Opéra (1er aspect) **Lost**
11. *Place du Théâtre-Français (Paris)*
    Place du Théâtre-Français **Lost**
12. *A Little Rascal*
    Un petit diable **Lost**
13. *Coronation of a Village Maiden (French customs)*
    Couronnement de la rosière **Lost**
14. *Baby and Young Girls*
    Bébé et Fillettes **Lost**
15. *Post No Bills*
    Défense d'afficher **Survives**
16. *Steamboats on River Seine*
    Bateaux-Mouches sur la Seine **Lost**
17. *Place de l'Opéra, 2d view (Paris)*
    Place de l'Opéra (2e aspect) **Lost**
18. *Boulevard des Italiens (Paris)*
    Boulevard des Italiens **Lost**
19. *Academy for Young Ladies*
    Un lycée de jeunes filles **Lost**
20. *Bois de Boulogne (Touring Club, Paris)*
    Bois de Boulogne (Touring Club) **Lost**
21. *Bois de Boulogne (Porte de Madrid, Paris)*
    Bois de Boulogne (Porte de Madrid) **Lost**
22. *The Rescue on the River (1st part)*
    Sauvetage en rivière (1re partie) **Lost**
23. *The Rescue on the River (2d part)*
    Sauvetage en rivière (2e partie) **Lost**
24. *French Regiment Going to the Parade*
    Le Régiment **Lost**
25. *Gipsies at Home*
    Campement de bohémiens **Lost**
26. *A Terrible Night*
    Une nuit terrible **Survives**
27. *Unloading the Boat (Havre)*
    Déchargement de bateaux (Le Havre) **Lost**
28. *The Beach at Villers in a Gale (France)*
    Plage de Villers par gros temps **Lost**
29. *The Docks at Marseilles (France)*
    Les Quais à Marseille **Lost**
30. *Beach and Pier at Trouville (France)*
    Jetée et plage de Trouville (1re partie) **Lost**
31. *Boat Leaving the Harbor of Trouville*
    Barque sortant du port de Trouville **Lost**
32. *Beach and Pier at Trouville (2d part)*
    Jetée et plage de Trouville (2e partie) **Lost**
33. *Market Day (Trouville)*
    Jour de marché à Trouville **Lost**
34. *Panorama of Havre Taken From a Boat*
    Panorama du Havre (pris d'un bateau) **Lost**

35.	*Arrival of a Train (Joinville Station)* *Arrivée d'un train (gare de Joinville)* **Lost**	54.	*Place de la Concorde (Paris)* *Place de la Concorde* **Lost**
36.	*A Soldier's Unlucky Salutation* *Salut malencontreux* Also known as *Salut malencontreux d'un déserteur* **Lost**	55.	*St. Lazare Railroad Station (Paris)* *La Gare Saint-Lazare* **Lost**
		56.	*Manoeuvres of the French Army* *Grandes Manœuvres* **Lost**
37.	*A Lightning Sketch (Mr. Thiers)* *Dessinateur express (M. Thiers)* **Lost**	57.	*A Lightning Sketch (Chamberlain)* *Dessinateur (Chamberlain)* **Lost**
38.	*Blacksmith in His Workshop* *Les Forgerons (vue d'atelier)* **Lost**	58.	*Place de la Bastille (Paris)* *Place de la Bastille* **Lost**
39.	*A Janitor in Trouble* *Tribulations d'un concierge* **Lost**	59.	*Tide Rising Over the Breakwater* *Marée montante sur brise-lames* **Lost**
40.	*Sea Bathing* *Baignade en mer* **Lost**	60.	*Return to the Barracks* *Retour au cantonnement* **Lost**
41.	*Children Playing on the Beach* *Enfants jouant sur la plage* **Lost**	61.	*A Lightning Sketch (H.M. Queen Victoria)* *Dessinateur (Reine Victoria)* **Lost**
42.	*Conjurer Making Ten Hats in Sixty Seconds* *Dix Chapeaux en soixante secondes* **Lost**	62.	*French Officers' Meeting* *Réunion d'officiers* **Lost**
43.	*Sea Breaking on the Rocks* *Effet de mer sur les rochers* **Lost**	63.	*The Pier at Tréport During a Storm (France)* *Tempête sur la jetée du Tréport* **Lost**
44.	*A Serpentine Dance* *Danse serpentine* **Lost**	64.	*The Bivouac* *Le Bivouac* **Lost**
45.	*Miss de Vère (English jig)* *Miss de Vère (gigue anglaise)* **Lost**	65.	*Threshing-Machine Worked by Power* also known as *Threshing Machines Worked by Power* *Batteuse à vapeur* **Lost**
46.	*Automobiles Starting on a Race* *Départ des automobiles* **Lost**		
47.	*A Naval Review at Cherbourg* *Revue navale à Cherbourg* **Lost**	66.	*Sacks Up!* *Sac au dos!* **Lost**
48.	*The Czar and His Cortège Going to Versailles* *Cortège du Tzar allant à Versailles* **Lost**	67.	*Breaking up of the Territorial Army (France)* *Libération des territoriaux* **Lost**
49.	*Towing a Boat on the River* *Les Haleurs de bateaux* **Lost**	68.	*Officers of French Army Leaving Service* *Départ des officiers* **Lost**
50.	*The Czar's Cortège in the Bois de Boulogne* *Cortège du Tzar au Bois de Boulogne* **Lost**	69.	*Place Saint-Augustin (Paris)* *Place Saint-Augustin* **Lost**
51.	*Closing Hours at Vibert's Perfume Factory (Paris)* *Sortie des ateliers Vibert* **Lost**	70.	*The Vanishing Lady* *Escamotage d'une dame chez Robert-Houdin* **Survives**
52.	*The Potter's Cart* *La Voiture du potier* **Lost**	71.	*The Fakir (a Hindoo mystery)* *Le Fakir (mystère indien)* **Lost**
53.	*The Mysterious Paper* *Le Papier protée* **Lost**	72.	*A Badly Managed Hotel* *L'Hôtel empoisonné* **Lost**

73.	*A Lightning Sketch (Von Bismarck)*		91.	*Firemen on Parade*
	Dessinateur (Von Bismarck) **Lost**			*Défilé des pompiers* **Lost**
74.	*The Peeping Toms*		92.	*Dancing Girls (Jardin de Paris)*
	Les Indiscrets **Lost**			*Danseuses au Jardin de Paris* **Lost**
75.	*Tom Old Boot (a grotesque dwarf)*		93.	*An Imaginary Patient*
	Tom Old Boot (nain grotesque) **Lost**			*Le Malade imaginaire* **Lost**
76.	*A Quarrel in a Café*		94.	*A Funny Mahometan*
	Une altercation au café **Lost**			*Le Musulman rigolo* **Lost**
77.	*The Drunkards*		95.	*An Hallucinated Alchemist*
	Les Ivrognes **Lost**			*L'Hallucination de l'alchimiste* **Lost**
			96.	*The Devil's Castle (US)*

1896–1897

78–80.	*The Haunted Castle (US)*
	The Devil's Castle (UK)
	Le Manoir du diable **Survives**
81.	*An Up-to-Date Dentist*
	Chicot, dentiste américain **Lost**
82.	*A Nightmare*
	Le Cauchemar **Survives**

1897

83–84.	*The Mardi Gras Procession (Paris, 1897)*
	Le Cortège du Bœuf gras passant place de la Concorde **Lost**
85.	*The Mardi Gras Procession (Paris, 1898)* [sic]
	Cortège du Bœuf gras, boulevard des Italiens **Lost**
86.	*A Farm Yard*
	Une cour de ferme **Lost**
87.	*Military Apprentices*
	Les Apprentis militaires **Lost**
88.	*Comedian Paulus Singing "Derrière l'Omnibus"*
	Paulus chantant: Derrière l'omnibus **Lost**
89.	*Comedian Paulus Singing "Coquin de Printemps"*
	Paulus chantant: Coquin de printemps **Lost**
90.	*Comedian Paulus Singing "Duelliste Marsellais"*
	Paulus chantant: Duelliste marseillais **Lost**

	The Haunted Castle (UK)
	Le Château hanté **Survives**
97–98.	*Mid-Lent Procession in Paris*
	Cortège de la Mi-Carême **Lost**
99.	*Battle With Confetti*
	Bataille de confettis **Lost**
100.	*On the Roofs*
	Sur les toits (cambrioleurs et gendarmes) **Survives**
101.	*D. Devant, Conjurer*
	D. Devant (prestidigitation) **Lost**
102.	*The School for Sons-in-law*
	L'École des gendres **Lost**
103–104.	*War Episodes*
	Épisode de guerre **Lost**
105.	*The Last Cartridges*
	Bombardement d'une maison (reconstitution de la scène des Dernières Cartouches) **Survives**
106.	*The Surrender of Tournavos*
	La Prise de Tournavos **Survives**
107.	*Execution of a Spy*
	Exécution d'un espion **Lost**
108.	*Massacre in Crete*
	Massacres en Crète **Lost**
109.	*A Dangerous Pass (Mont Blanc)*
	Passage dangereux (Mont-Blanc) **Lost**
110.	*Sea Fighting in Greece*
	Combat naval en Grèce **Survives**
111.	*Gugusse and the Automaton*
	Gugusse et l'Automate **Lost**

112.	*Between Dover and Calais* also known as *Between Calais and Dover* *Entre Calais et Douvres* **Survives**	135.	*Attack of an English Blockhouse* *Attaque d'un poste anglais* **Lost**
113.	*Peeping Tom at the Seaside* *L'Indiscret aux bains de mer* **Lost**	136.	*Boxing Match* *Match de boxe (professeurs de l'École de Joinville)* **Lost**
114.	*Behind the Scenes* *Dans les coulisses (scène comique dans un théâtre)* **Lost**	137.	*A Drunkard's Dream* *Vision d'ivrogne* **Lost**
115.	*A Potterymaker* *Tourneur en poterie* **Lost**	**1897–1898**	
116.	*The Grasshopper and the Ant* *La Cigale et la Fourmi* **Lost**	138.	*Faust and Marguerite* *Faust et Marguerite* **Lost**
117.	*A Balloon Ascension (very comical)* *Ascension d'un ballon* **Lost**	139.	*Place de l'Opéra, 3d view (Paris)* *Carrefour de l'Opéra* **Lost**
118–120.	*Laboratory of Mephistopheles* *Le Cabinet de Méphistophélès* **Lost**	140–141.	*Black Art (US)* *Devilish Magic (UK)* *Magie diabolique* **Lost**
121.	*The Barber and the Farmer* *Figaro et l'Auvergnat* **Survives**	**1898**	
122–123.	*The Bewitched Inn* *L'Auberge ensorcelée* **Survives**	142.	*A Novice at X-Rays* *Les Rayons X* **Lost**
124.	*Auguste and Bibb* *Auguste et Bibb* **Lost**	143.	*Collision and Shipwreck at Sea* *Collision et Naufrage en mer* **Lost**
125.	*A Twentieth Century Surgeon* *Chirurgien américain* **Lost**	144–145.	*The Blowing up of the "Maine" in Havana Harbor* *Quais de La Havane (Explosion du cuirassé Le Maine)* **Lost**
126.	*The Charcoal Man's Reception* *Arlequin et Charbonnier* **Lost**	146.	*A View of the Wreck of the "Maine"* *Visite de l'épave du Maine* **Lost**
127.	*A Private Dinner* *En cabinet particulier* **Lost**	147.	*Divers at Work on the Wreck of the "Maine" (US)* *Divers at Work on a Wreck Under Sea (UK)* *Visite sous-marine du Maine (plongeurs et poissons vivants)* **Survives**
128.	*After the Ball* *Après le bal (le tub)* **Survives**		
129.	*A Hypnotist at Work (US)* *While Under a Hypnotist's Influence (UK)* *Le Magnétiseur* **Lost**	148.	*Fencing at the Joinville School* *Assaut d'escrime (École de Joinville)* **Lost**
130–131.	*An Irritable Model* *Le Modèle irascible* **Lost**	149.	*A Clumsy Mason* *Le Maçon maladroit* **Lost**
132.	*Dancing in a Harem* *Danse au sérail* **Unknown**	150.	*Defending the Fort at Manila (US)* *Defending the Fort (UK)* *Combat naval devant Manille* **Lost**
133.	*Slave Trading in a Harem* *Vente d'esclaves au harem* **Lost**		
134.	*Fighting in the Streets in India* *Combat dans une rue aux Indes* **Lost**		

151.	*Panorama from Top of Moving Train* also known as *Panorama from Top of a Moving Train* *Panorama pris d'un train en marche (ponts et tunnels)* **Survives**	163.	*West Point* also known as *Fresh Paint* *Prenez garde à la peinture* **Lost**
152.	*A Soldier's Tedious Duty* *Corvée de quartier accidentée* **Lost**	164.	*The Cave of the Demons* *La Caverne maudite* **Lost**
153.	*The Magician (US)* *Black Magic (UK)* *Le Magicien* **Survives**	165.	*The Artist's Dream* *Rêve d'artiste* **Lost**
154.	*A Soldier's French Leave* *Sorti sans permission* **Lost**	166.	*The Painter's Studio* *Atelier d'artiste (farce de modèles)* **Lost**
155.	*The Famous Box Trick* *Illusions fantasmagoriques* **Survives**	167.	*The Four Troublesome Heads* *Un homme de têtes* also known as *Un homme de tête* **Survives**
156.	*Pygmalion and Galatea* *Pygmalion et Galathée* **Survives**	168.	*The Cripple Lady (US)* *The Triple Lady (UK)* *Dédoublement cabalistique* **Lost**
157.	*Shooting the Chutes* *Montagnes russes nautiques* **Lost**		
158.	*Damnation of Faust* *Damnation de Faust* **Lost**		

1898–1899

159.	*Adventures of William Tell* *Guillaume Tell et le Clown* **Survives**
160–162.	*The Astronomer's Dream, or the Man in the Moon* *La Lune à un mètre (1—l'observatoire; 2—la Lune; 3—Phœbé)* also known as *L'Homme dans la Lune* **Survives**

169.	*Temptation of St. Anthony* *Tentation de saint Antoine* **Survives**
170.	*The Beggar's Dream* *Rêve du pauvre* **Lost**
171.	*A Dinner Under Difficulties* *Salle à manger fantastique* **Survives**

1899

172.	*Fantastical Illusions* *Création spontanée* also known as *Illusions fantastiques* **Lost**
173–174.	*Funeral of Felix Faure* *Funérailles de Félix Faure (1—char; 2—les troupes)* **Lost**
175–176.	*Robbing Cleopatra's Tomb* *Le Sacrilège (1—l'attentat; 2—résurrection de Cléopâtre)* also known as *Cléopâtre* **Unknown**
177–178.	*The Bridegroom's Dilemma* *Le Coucher de la mariée ou Triste nuit de noces* advertised as a *scène comique* **Lost**
179.	*A Political Duel* *Duel politique* **Lost**
180.	*An Extraordinary Wrestling Match* *Luttes extravagantes* **Survives**

181.	*The Wandering Minstrel* *Richesse et Misère ou la Cigale et la Fourmi* **Lost**	197.	*Absent-Minded Lecturer* *Le Conférencier distrait* **Lost**
182.	*The Sentry's Stratagem* *L'Ours et la Sentinelle* **Lost**	198.	*The Philosopher's Stone* *La Pierre philosophale* **Lost**
183.	*An Up-to-Date Conjurer (US)* *An Up-to-Date Conjuror (UK)* also known as *The Conjurer (English)* and *L'Impressionniste fin de siècle (French)* *L'Illusionniste fin de siècle* **Survives**	199.	*Cagliostro's Mirror* *Le Miroir de Cagliostro (miroir avec apparitions mystérieuses)* **Lost**
		200.	*Neptune and Amphitrite* *Neptune et Amphitrite (illusion mythologique sur mer)* **Lost**
		201.	*Bird's-Eye View of St. Helier (Jersey)* *Panorama du port de Saint-Hélier (île de Jersey)* **Lost**
184.	*Murder Will Out* *Le Spectre* **Lost**	202.	*Steamer Entering the Harbor of Jersey* *Entrée du paquebot Victoria dans le port de Jersey* **Lost**
185–187.	*The Devil in a Convent (US)* *"The Sign of the Cross", or the Devil in a Convent (UK)* *Le Diable au couvent (1. Les nonnes, le sermon. 2. Les démons, le sabbat. 3. Le clergé, l'exorcisme)* **Survives**	203.	*Passengers Landing at Harbor of Granville* *Débarquement des voyageurs, port de Granville* **Lost**
		204.	*Christ Walking on the Water* *Le Christ marchant sur les flots (exécuté sur mer véritable)* **Lost**
188.	*Haggard's "She"—The Pillar of Fire* *Danse du feu* **Survives**	205.	*Summoning the Spirits* *Évocation spirite* advertised as a *scène à transformations* **Survives**
189.	*The Spanish Inquisition—Cremation* *La Crémation (le supplice, le miracle)* **Lost**	206.	*Dreyfus Court Martial—Arrest of Dreyfus (US)* *Arrest of Dreyfus, 1894 (UK)* *Dictée du bordereau (arrestation de Dreyfus)* **Survives**
190.	*A Midnight Episode* *Un bon lit* **Unknown**		
191.	*The Slippery Burglar* *Force doit rester à la loi* **Lost**		
192.	*A Drop Too Much* *Pickpocket et Policeman* **Lost**	207.	*Devil's Island—Within the palisade (US)* *Dreyfus at Devil's Island—Within the palisade (UK)* *La Case de Dreyfus à l'île du Diable* **Survives**
193.	*A Lively Cock-Fight (US)* *A Lively Cock Fight (UK)* *Combat de coqs* **Lost**		
194–195.	*The Clown and Automobile (US)* *The Clown and Motor Car (UK)* *Automaboulisme et Autorité (scène comique clownesque)* **Fragment**	208.	*Dreyfus Put in Irons (US)* *Dreyfus Put in Irons—Inside Cell at Devil's Island (UK)* *Dreyfus mis aux fers (la double boucle)* **Survives**
196.	*A Mysterious Portrait* also known as *The Mysterious Portrait* *Le Portrait mystérieux (grande nouveauté photographique extraordinaire)* **Survives**	209.	*Suicide of Colonel Henry* *Suicide du colonel Henry* **Survives**

210. *Landing of Dreyfus at Quiberon* (US)
Landing of Dreyfus from Devil's Island (UK)
Débarquement de Dreyfus à Quiberon **Survives**

211. *Dreyfus Meets His Wife at Rennes* (US)
Dreyfus in Prison of Rennes (UK)
Entrevue de Dreyfus et de sa femme (prison de Rennes) **Survives**

212. *The Attempt Against the Life of Maitre Labori* (US)
The Attempt Against Maitre Labori (UK)
Attentat contre Me Labori **Survives**

213. *The Fight of Reporters at the Lycée* (US)
The Fight of Journalists at the Lycee (UK)
Suspension d'audience (bagarre entre journalistes) **Survives**

214–215. *The Court Martial at Rennes*
Le Conseil de guerre en séance à Rennes **Survives**

216. *The Degradation of Dreyfus* (US)
The Degradation of Dreyfus in 1894 (UK)
La Dégradation **Survives**

217. *Dreyfus Leaving the Lycée for Jail* (US)
Officers and Dreyfus Leaving the Lycee (UK)
Dreyfus allant du lycée de Rennes à la prison **Survives**

218. *The Human Pyramid*
La Pyramide de Triboulet advertised as a *tableau sensationnel pour coloris* **Survives**

219–224. *Cinderella*
Cendrillon **Survives**

225. *The Snow Man*
La Statue de neige advertised as a *scène comique* **Lost**

226–227. *The Mysterious Knight*
Le Chevalier mystère **Survives**

228–229. *The Lightning Change Artist* (US)
The Chameleon Man (UK)
L'Homme protée **Lost**

230–231. *The Interrupted Honeymoon*
Charmant voyage de noces **Lost**

232. *Panorama of River Seine*
Panorama de la Seine (les travaux de l'exposition de 1900: le Vieux-Paris, rive droite) **Lost**

233. *Panorama of River Seine*
Panorama de la Seine (les travaux de l'exposition de 1900: les palais en construction, rive gauche) **Lost**

1899–1900

234. *Addition and Subtraction*
Tom Whisky ou l'Illusionniste toqué **Survives**

235. *The Railroad Pickpocket* may have been released in the UK as *The Railway Pickpocket*
Fatale Méprise (scène comique en wagon) **Lost**

236. *An Intruder Behind the Scenes*
Un intrus dans une loge de figurantes **Lost**

237–240. *The Miracles of Brahmin* (US)
The Miracles of the Brahmin (UK)
Les Miracles du Brahmine **Survives**

1900

241. *Scullion's Joke on the Chef*
Farces de marmitons **Lost**

242. *The Three Bacchants* (US)
The Three Bacchantes (UK)
Les Trois Bacchantes **Lost**

243. *The Cook's Revenge*
La Vengeance du gâte-sauce **Survives**

244. *The Misfortunes of an Explorer*
Les Infortunes d'un explorateur ou les Momies récalcitrantes **Survives**

245. *Paris Exposition, 1900—"La Porte Monumentale"*
La Porte Monumentale **Unknown**

246. *Paris Exposition, 1900—Moving Panorama, 1*
Panorama mouvant pris du trottoir roulant (le Champ-de-Mars) **Unknown**

247.	*Paris Exposition, 1900—Moving Panorama, 2* *Panorama mouvant pris du trottoir roulant (l'esplanade des Invalides)* **Unknown**	257.	*Paris Exposition, 1900—Panoramic Circular Tour; "Les Invalides"* *Panorama circulaire (les Invalides)* **Unknown**
248.	*Paris Exposition, 1900—Moving Panorama, 3* *Panorama mouvant pris du trottoir roulant (la rue des Nations)* **Unknown**	258.	*Paris Exposition, 1900—Circular Panorama; Champ de Mars* *Panorama circulaire (pris du centre du Champ-de-Mars)* **Unknown**
249.	*Paris Exposition, 1900—Details Connected With the Moving Sidewalk* *Détail du trottoir roulant* **Unknown**	259.	*Paris Exposition, 1900—Trocadero* *Panorama circulaire (pris du centre du jardin du Trocadéro)* **Unknown**
250.	*Paris Exposition, 1900—The Moving Sidewalk* *La Plate-forme roulante* **Unknown**	260.	*Paris Exposition, 1900—Iéna Bridge* *Panorama circulaire de la Seine (pont d'Iéna)* **Unknown**
251.	*Paris Exposition, 1900—Panoramic View, taken while boating on the River Seine.—Army and Navy Pavilions* *Vue panoramique prise en bateau sur la Seine (le pavillon des armées de Terre et de Mer)* **Unknown**	261.	*Paris Exposition, 1900—From the Trocadero* *Panorama semi-circulaire (pris du sommet des tours du Trocadéro)* **Unknown**
252.	*Paris Exposition, 1900—Panoramic View, taken while boating on the River Seine.—Foreign palaces* *Vue panoramique faisant suite à la précédente (les palais étrangers)* **Unknown**	262–263.	*The One Man Band* *L'Homme-Orchestre* **Survives**
253.	*Paris Exposition, 1900—Panoramic View, taken while boating on the River Seine.—Old Paris* *Vue panoramique prise en bateau sur la Seine (panorama général du Vieux Paris)* **Unknown**		
254.	*Paris Exposition, 1900—The Avenue of the Champs Elysées.—Palaces of Fine Arts* *Porte d'entrée de l'Exposition sur l'avenue des Champs-Élysées* **Unknown**	264–275.	*Joan of Arc* *Jeanne d'Arc* **Fragment**
255.	*Paris Exposition, 1900—Panoramic View from the Electric Railway* *Vue panoramique prise à l'avant du train électrique* **Unknown**	276–278.	*The Seven Capital Sins* *Les Sept Péchés capitaux* **Lost**
		279.	*The Tricky Prisoner* *Le Prisonnier récalcitrant* **Lost**
256.	*Paris Exposition, 1900—Panoramic Excursion Round the Champs Elysées* *Panorama circulaire des Champs-Élysées (Palais des Beaux-Arts)* **Unknown**	280.	Unknown title
		281–282.	*The Rajah's Dream, or the Bewitched Wood* *Le Rêve du Radjah ou la Forêt enchantée* **Survives**

283. The Two Blind Men
Les Deux Aveugles **Lost**
284. The Artist and the Mannikin
L'Artiste et le Mannequin **Survives**
285–286. The Wizard, the Prince and the Good Fairy (US)
The Sorcerer, the Prince, and the Good Fairy (UK)
Le Sorcier, le Prince et le Bon Génie **Survives**
287. Don't Move
Ne bougeons plus! **Lost**
288. The Dangerous Lunatic
Le Fou assassin **Lost**
289–291. The Magic Book
Le Livre magique **Survives**
292. Thanking the Audience
Vue de remerciements au Public **Lost**
293. The Up-to-Date Spiritualism
Spiritisme abracadabrant **Survives**
294. The Triple Conjuror and the Living Head
L'Illusioniste double et la Tête vivante **Survives**
295–297. The Miser's Dream of Gold (US)
The Miser, or the Gold Country (UK)
Le Songe d'or de l'avare **Lost**
298–305. The Christmas Dream
Rêve de Noël advertised as a *féerie cinématographique à grand spectacle en 20 tableaux* **Survives**
306. Crying and Laughing
Gens qui pleurent et Gens qui rient **Unknown**
307–308. Coppelia, the Animated Doll
Coppelia ou la Poupée animée **Lost**
309–310. Fat and Lean Wrestling Match (US)
The Wrestling Sextette (UK)
Nouvelles Luttes extravagantes **Survives**
311. A Fantastical Meal
Le Repas fantastique **Survives**
312–313. Going to Bed Under Difficulties (US)
An Increasing Wardrobe (UK)
Le Déshabillage impossible **Survives**
314. Eight Girls in a Barrel (US)
The Danaid's Barrel (UK)
Le Tonneau des Danaïdes **Survives**
315. The Man With Wheels in His Head (US)
The Gouty Patient (UK)
Le Malade hydrophobe **Unknown**
316. Practical Joke in a Bar Room (US)
A Practical Joke in a Bar Room (UK)
Une mauvaise plaisanterie **Lost**
317. The Doctor and the Monkey
Le Savant et le Chimpanzé **Survives**
318–319. The Conjurer With Hundred Tricks (US)
The Conjuror With a Hundred Tricks (UK)
L'Homme aux cent trucs **Lost**
320–321. The Clown Versus Satan
Guguste et Belzébuth **Lost**
322. How He Missed His Train
Le Réveil d'un monsieur pressé **Survives**
323–324. Twentieth Century Surgery
La Chirurgie de l'avenir **Lost**
325–326. What Is Home Without the Boarder
La Maison tranquille advertised as a *scène comique* **Survives**
327. China Versus Allied Powers (US)
China Versus the Allied Nations (UK)
Le Congrès des Nations en Chine **Lost**
328. The Balloonist's Mishap
Les Mésaventures d'un aéronaute **Lost**
329–331. The Bewitched Dungeon
La Tour maudite advertised with the subtitle *Transformations* **Lost** — Untitled advertising films **Lost**

1900–1901

332–333. The Brahmin and the Butterfly
La Chrysalide et le Papillon d'or also known as Le Brahmane et le Papillon **Survives**
334. The Triple-Headed Lady
Bouquet d'illusions **Survives**
335–336. Dislocation Extraordinary also known as Extraordinary Illusions
Dislocation mystérieuse **Survives**

337–344.	Red Riding Hood *Le Petit Chaperon rouge* advertised as a *pièce féerique à grand spectacle en 12 tableaux* **Lost**	373.	A Phrenological Burlesque (US) The Phrenologist and the Lively Skull (UK) *Phrénologie burlesque* **Lost**
		374–375.	The Dragon Fly *La Libellule* **Lost**
1901		376–378.	The Trials of a Schoolmaster *L'École infernale* **Lost**
345–347.	The Magician's Cavern (US) The Magician's Cavern/The House of Mystery (UK) *L'Antre des esprits* **Survives**	379–380.	The Dream of a Hindu Beggar *Le Rêve du paria (sujet artistique)* **Lost**
		381.	The Elastic Battalion *Le Bataillon élastique (cocasserie fantastique)* **Lost**
348–349.	A Maiden's Paradise *Le Chimiste repopulateur* **Lost**		
350–351.	The Bachelor's Paradise *Chez la sorcière* **Survives**	382–383.	The Man With the Rubber Head (US) A Swelled Head (UK) *L'Homme à la tête en caoutchouc* **Survives**
352–353.	The Temple of the Sun *Le Temple de la Magie* **Lost**		
354.	Painless Dentistry (US) Harmless Dentistry (UK) *Le Charlatan* **Unknown**	**1901–1902**	
		384–385.	The Devil and the Statue (US) The Gigantic Devil (UK) *Le Diable géant ou le Miracle de la Madone* advertised as a *grande nouveauté* **Survives**
355.	Fun in Court (US) Contempt of Court (UK) *Une noce au village* **Lost**		
356.	A Good Trick (US) The Fierce Charger and the Knight (UK) *Le Chevalier démontable et le Général Boum* **Lost**	386.	The Dwarf and the Giant (US) The Long and Short of It (UK) *Nain et Géant* **Survives**
		387–389.	The Cabinet Trick of the Davenport Brothers (US) The Mysterious Cabinet (UK) *L'Armoire des frères Davenport* **Lost**
357–358.	Excelsior! (US) The Prince of Magicians (UK) *Excelsior!* **Survives**		
359.	Off to Bloomingdale Asylum (US) Off to Bedlam (UK) *L'Omnibus des toqués ou Blancs et Noirs* also known as *Échappés de Charenton* **Survives**		
360.	The Sacred Fountain *La Fontaine sacrée ou la Vengeance de Bouddha* **Lost**		
361–370.	Blue Beard *Barbe-Bleue* **Survives**		
371–372.	A Hat With Many Surprises (US) The Hat of Many Surprises (UK) *Le Chapeau à surprises* **Survives**		

1902

390.	Wine Cellar Burglars (US) The Burglars in the Wine Cellar (UK) Les Piqueurs de fûts **Lost**
391.	The Colonel's Shower Bath (US) The Painter's Mishap in the Barracks (UK) Douche du colonel **Survives**
392–393.	Prolific Magical Egg (US) The Egg in Black Art (UK) L'Œuf du sorcier also known as L'Oeuf Magique Prolifique **Survives**
394–396.	The Dancing Midget (US) Marvellous Egg Producing With Surprising Developments (UK) La Danseuse microscopique **Survives**
397.	The Eruption of Mount Pelee (US) The Terrible Eruption of Mount Pelée and Destruction of St. Pierre, Martinique (UK) Éruption volcanique à la Martinique **Survives**
398.	The Catastrophe of the Balloon "Le Pax" Catastrophe du Ballon Le Pax **Lost**
399–411.	A Trip to the Moon (US) Trip to the Moon (UK) Voyage dans la Lune **Survives**
412.	The Shadow-Girl (US) Twentieth Century Conjuring (UK) La Clownesse fantôme **Survives**
Urban.	The Coronation of Edward VII Le Sacre d'Édouard VII **Survives**
413–414.	The Treasures of Satan (US) The Devil's Money Bags (UK) Les Trésors de Satan **Survives**
415–416.	The Human Fly L'Homme-Mouche **Survives**
417–418.	Marvellous Suspension and Evolution (US) Marvellous Suspension and Evolutions (UK) La Femme volante **Survives**
419.	An Impossible Balancing Feat (US) An Impossible Feat of Balancing (UK) L'Équilibre impossible **Survives**
420–421.	Drunkard and Inventor (US) What Befell the Inventor's Visitor (UK) Le Pochard et l'Inventeur **Lost**
422–425.	Up-to-Date Surgery (US) Sure Cure for Indigestion (UK) Une indigestion advertised as a scène comique; also known as Chirurgie fin de siècle **Survives**
426–429.	Gulliver's Travels Among the Lilliputians and the Giants (US) Gulliver's Travels—In the land of the Lilliputians and the Giants (UK) Le Voyage de Gulliver à Lilliput et chez les Géants also known as Voyages de Gulliver **Survives**
430–443.	Robinson Crusoe Les Aventures de Robinson Crusoé **Fragment**

1902–1903

444.	The Enchanted Basket La Corbeille enchantée **Unknown**
445–448.	The Marvellous Wreath (US) The Marvellous Hoop (UK) La Guirlande merveilleuse **Survives**
449–450.	Beelzebub's Daughters (US) The Women of Fire (UK) Les Filles du diable **Unknown**
451–452.	Misfortune Never Comes Alone (US) Accidents Never Happen Singly (UK) Un malheur n'arrive jamais seul **Survives**

1903

453–457.	The Cake Walk Infernal (US) The Infernal Cake Walk (UK) Le Cake-Walk infernal **Survives**
458–459.	The Mysterious Box (US) The Shallow Trick Box (UK) also known as The Shallow Box Trick La Boîte à malice **Survives**

460–461.	The Queen's Musketeers (US) The Musketeers of the Queen (UK) Les Mousquetaires de la reine **Lost**	483–498.	Fairyland, or the Kingdom of the Fairies (US) The Wonders of the Deep, or Kingdom of the Fairies (UK) also known as The Kingdom of the Fairies Le Royaume des fées **Survives**
462–464.	The Enchanted Well Le Puits fantastique **Survives**		
465–469.	The Inn Where No Man Rests (US) The Inn of "Good Rest" (UK) L'Auberge du bon repos **Survives**	499–500.	The Infernal Caldron and the Phantasmal Vapors (US) The Infernal Cauldron (UK) Le Chaudron infernal **Survives**
470–471.	The Drawing Lesson, or the Living Statue La Statue animée advertised as a scène Louis XV à trucs **Survives**	501–502.	The Apparition, or Mr. Jones' Comical Experience With a Ghost (US) The Ghost and the Candle (UK) also known as Apparitions Le Revenant **Survives**
		503–505.	Jupiter's Thunderbolts, or the Home of the Muses also known as Jupiter's Thunderballs Le Tonnerre de Jupiter **Survives**
		506–507.	Ten Ladies in One Umbrella (US) Ten Girls in One Umbrella (UK) also known as Ten Ladies in an Umbrella La Parapluie fantastique **Survives**
		508–509.	Jack Jaggs and Dum Dum (US) The Rival Music Hall Artistes (UK) Tom Tight et Dum Dum **Survives**
		510–511.	Bob Kick, the Mischievous Kid Bob Kick, l'enfant terrible **Survives**
472.	The Mystical Flame La Flamme merveilleuse **Survives**	512–513.	Extraordinary Illusions (US) The 20th Century Illustrationist (UK) Illusions funambulesques **Survives**
473–475.	The Witch's Revenge (US) The Sorcerer's Revenge (UK) Le Sorcier **Survives**	514–516.	Alcofrisbas, the Master Magician (US) The Enchanter (UK) L'Enchanteur Alcofribas **Survives**
476.	The Oracle of Delphi L'Oracle de Delphes **Survives**	517–519.	Jack and Jim Comical Conjuring (UK) Jack et Jim **Survives**
477–478.	A Spiritualistic Photographer Le Portrait spirite **Survives**	520–524.	The Magic Lantern (US) The Magic Lantern, or the Bioscope in the Toy Shop (UK) La Lanterne magique **Survives**
479–480.	The Melomaniac Le Mélomane **Survives**		
481–482.	The Monster Le Monstre **Survives**	525–526.	The Ballet-Master's Dream (US) The Dream of the Ballet Master (UK) Le Rêve du maître de ballet **Survives**

527–533.	*The Damnation of Faust* (US) *The Condemnation of Faust* (UK) *Faust aux enfers* **Survives**	545.	*Every Man His Own Cigar Lighter* *Un peu de feu, S.V.P.* **Fragment**
534–535.	*The Terrible Turkish Executioner, or It Served Him Right* (US) *What Befell the Turkish Executioner* (UK) *Le Bourreau turc* **Survives**	546.	*The Invisible Siva* (US) *The Invisible Sylvia* [sic] (UK) *Siva l'invisible* **Lost**
536–537.	*A Burlesque Highway Robbery in "Gay Paree"* (US) *The "Apaches"—Parisian hooligans* (UK) *Les Apaches* **Lost**	547–549.	*The Bewitched Trunk* (US) *The Enchanted Trunk* (UK) *Le Coffre enchanté (scène merveilleuse et comique)* **Survives**
		550–551.	*The Fugitive Apparitions* (US) *Short Lived Apparitions* (UK) *Les Apparitions fugitives* **Survives**
		552–553.	*The Untamable Whiskers* (US) *The King of the Mackerel Fishers* (UK) *Le Roi du maquillage* **Survives**
		554–555.	*The Clockmaker's Dream* (US) *The Dream of the Clock Maker* (UK) *Le Rêve de l'horloger* **Survives**
		556–557.	*The Imperceptible Transmutations* (US) *Imperceptible Transformation* (UK) *Les Transmutations imperceptibles* **Survives**
		558–559.	*A Miracle Under the Inquisition* (US) *A Miracle of the Inquisition* (UK) *Un miracle sous l'inquisition* **Survives**
538–539.	*A Moonlight Serenade, or the Miser Punished* (US) *Pierrot and the Moon* (UK) *Au clair de la Lune ou Pierrot malheureux* **Survives**	560–561.	*Benvenuto Cellini, or A Curious Evasion* (US) *Benvenuto Cellini, or the Curious Elopement* (UK) *Benvenuto Cellini ou Curieuse Évasion* **Survives**
1904		562–574.	*Faust and Marguerite* (US) *Faust* (UK) *Damnation du docteur Faust* **Survives**
540–541.	*Tit for Tat, or a Good Joke With My Head* (US) *"Tit for Tat"—The head in a case* (UK) *Un prêté pour un rendu (une bonne farce avec ma tête)* **Survives**	575–577.	*The Fake Russian Prophet* (US) *The Merry Prophet of Russia* (UK) *Le Joyeux Prophète russe (fantaisie russo-japonaise)* **Lost**
542–544.	*A Wager Between Two Magicians, or Jealous of Myself* (US) *A Juggling Contest Between Two Magicians* (UK) *Match de prestidigitation* **Survives**	578–580.	*Tchin-Chao, the Chinese Conjurer* (US) *The Chinese Juggler* (UK) *Le Thaumaturge chinois* **Survives**

581–584.	*The Wonderful Living Fan* (US) *The Wonderful Living Fan—Fine* (UK) *Le Merveilleux Éventail vivant* **Survives**	634–636.	*The Wonderful Rose-Tree* (US) *The Magical Rose Tree* (UK) *Le Rosier miraculeux* **Survives**
585–588.	*The Cook in Trouble* (US) *Cookery Bewitched* (UK) *Sorcellerie culinaire (scène clownesque)* **Survives**	637–638.	*The Shadow Lady* (US) *The Enchanted Cupboard* (UK) *La Dame fantôme* **Lost**
589–590.	*The Devilish Plank* (US) *The Devil's Plank* (UK) *La Planche du diable* **Survives**	639–640.	*A Wedding by Correspondence* (US) *Marriage by Correspondence* (UK) *Mariage par correspondance* **Lost**
591–592.	*The Impossible Dinner* (US) *The Impossible Dinner—Burlesque* (UK) *Le Dîner impossible* **Lost**	641–659.	*An Impossible Voyage* (US) *Whirling the Worlds* (UK) also known as *The Impossible Voyage* *Voyage à travers l'impossible* **Survives**
593–595.	*The Mermaid* *La Sirène* **Survives**	660–661.	*Supplementary Section of the "Impossible Voyage"* *Supplément Voyage à travers l'impossible* **Unknown**
596–597.	*The Mischances of a Drunkard* (US) *The Drunkard's Mishaps* (UK) *Les Mésaventures de M. Boit-sans-Soif* **Survives**	662–664.	*The Wandering Jew* *Le Juif errant* **Survives**
598–602.	*The Providence of the Waves, or the Dream of a Poor Fisherman* (US) *The Fisher's Guardian Angel* (UK) *La Providence de Notre-Dame-des-Flots* **Lost**	665–667.	*The Firefall* (US) *Cascade of Fire* (UK) *La Cascade de feu* **Survives**
603–605.	*Uncle Rube's Birthday (most comical and amusing)* (US) *Practical Joke on a Yokel* (UK) *La Fête au père Mathieu* **Lost**	668.	*The Grotto of Surprises* (US) *Grotto of Surprises* (UK) *La Grotte aux surprises* **Lost**
606–625.	*The Barber of Sevilla* also known as *The Barber of Sevilla, or the Useless Precaution* and *The Barber of Seville* *Le Barbier de Séville* **Lost**	669–677.	*The Christmas Angel* (US) *The Beggar Maiden* (UK) *Détresse et Charité* also known as *L'Ange de Noël* **Survives**
		1905	
626–627.	*The Animated Costumes* (US) *Animated Costumes* (UK) *Les Costumes animés* **Lost**	678–679.	*The Living Playing Cards* *Les Cartes vivantes* **Survives**
628–631.	*Simple Simon's Surprise Party* (US) *Bill Bailey's Dinner* (UK) *Les Invités de M. Latourte* also known as *Une Bonne Surprise* **Lost**	680–682.	*The King of Sharpshooters* *Le Roi des tireurs* **Lost**
		683–685.	*The Black Imp* *Le Diable noir* **Survives**
632–633.	*The Astonishing Frame* (US) *The Magic Frame* (UK) *Le Cadre aux surprises* **Lost**	686–689.	*The Crystal Casket* also known as *The Magic Dice* *Le Phénix ou le Coffret de cristal* **Fragment**

690–692.	*The Lilliputian Minuet* / *Le Menuet lilliputien* **Fragment**	784–785.	*The Scheming Gambler's Paradise* / *Le Tripot clandestin* **Survives**
693–695.	*A Mesmerian Experiment* / *Le Baquet de Mesmer* **Survives**	786–788.	*The Inventor Crazybrains and His Wonderful Airship* (US) / *Fantastical Air Ship* (UK) / *Le Dirigeable fantastique ou le Cauchemar d'un inventeur* **Survives**
696–698.	*Mr. Dauber and the Whimsical Picture* / *Le Peintre Barbouillard et le Tableau diabolique* **Lost**		

1906

699–701.	*The Venetian Looking-Glass* / *Le Miroir de Venise* advertised as *une mésaventure de Schylock* **Lost**
789–790.	*A Mix-up in the Gallery* / *Une chute de cinq étages* **Survives**
702–704.	*The Chloroform Fiends* / *Les Chevaliers du chloroforme* advertised as a *scène burlesque* **Lost**
791–806.	*Chimney Sweep* / *Jack le ramoneur* **Fragment**
705–726.	*The Palace of the Arabian Nights* / *Le Palais des mille et une nuits* **Survives**
807–809.	*Professor Do-mi-sol-do, the Luny Musician* / *Le Maestro Do-Mi-Sol-Do* **Survives**
727–731.	*A Crazy Composer* / *Le Compositeur toqué* **Survives**
810–812.	*Old and New Style Conjurers* / *La Magie à travers les âges* **Lost**
732–737.	*The Tower of London* / *Le Tour de Londres ou les Derniers Moments d'Anne de Boleyn* **Lost**
813–817.	*Who Looks, Pays!* / *L'Honneur est satisfait* **Lost**
738–739.	*The Enchanted Sedan Chair* / *La Chaise à porteurs enchantée* **Survives**
818–820.	*The Tramp and the Mattress Makers* / *La Cardeuse de matelas* **Survives**
740–749.	*An Adventurous Automobile Trip* / *Le Raid Paris–Monte-Carlo en automobile* also known as *Le Raid Paris–Monte-Carlo en deux heures* **Survives**
821–823.	*The Hilarious Posters* / *Les Affiches en goguette* **Survives**
824–837.	*A Desperate Crime* / *Les Incendiaires* also known as *Histoire d'un crime* **Fragment**
750–752.	*The Mysterious Island* / *L'Île de Calypso* advertised with the subtitle *Ulysse et le géant Polyphème* **Survives**
838–839.	*Punch and Judy* / *L'Anarchie chez Guignol* **Fragment**
840–842.	*A Spiritualist Meeting* / *Le Fantôme d'Alger* **Lost**
753–755.	*Unexpected Fireworks* / *Un feu d'artifice improvisé* **Survives**
843–845.	*A Roadside Inn* / *L'Hôtel des voyageurs de commerce ou les Suites d'une bonne cuite* **Survives**
756–775.	*Rip's Dream* / *La Légende de Rip Van Vinckle* [sic] **Survives**
846–848.	*Soap Bubbles* / *Les Bulles de savon animées* **Survives**
776–779.	*The Angler's Nightmare, or A Policeman's Troubles* / *Le Cauchemar du pêcheur ou l'Escarpolette fantastique* **Lost**
849–870.	*The Merry Frolics of Satan* / *Les Quat'Cents Farces du diable* **Survives**
871–873.	*A Seaside Flirtation* / *Le Rastaquouère Rodriguez y Papaguanas* **Lost**
780–783.	*Life-Saving Up-to-Date* / *Le Système du docteur Souflamort* **Lost**

874–876.	The Mysterious Retort (US) The Alchemist and the Demon (UK) L'Alchimiste Parafaragaramus ou la Cornue infernale **Survives**	961–968.	The Eclipse also known as The Eclipse, or the Courtship of the Sun and the Moon Éclipse du Soleil en pleine Lune **Survives**
877–887.	The Witch La Fée Carabosse ou le Poignard fatal advertised as a grande légende fantastique bretonne en 20 tableaux **Survives**	969–973.	The Bewildering Cabinet Le Placard infernal **Lost**
		974–979.	Chopin's Funeral March Burlesqued (US) Oh, That Band (UK) La Marche funèbre de Chopin **Lost**
888–905.	Robert Macaire and Bertrand Robert Macaire et Bertrand, les rois de cambrioleurs **Survives**	980–987.	Hamlet Prince of Denmark Hamlet **Lost**
—.	No English release Vers les étoiles **Lost**	988–994.	A Forester Made King Bernard le bûcheron ou le Miracle de saint Hubert **Lost**
1907		995–999.	Shakespeare Writing "Julius Caesar" La Mort de Jules César (Shakespeare) **Lost**
906–908.	A Mischievous Sketch Le Carton fantastique **Lost**		
909–911.	Rogues' Tricks (US) The Burglar's Bath (UK) La Douche d'eau bouillante **Survives**	1000–1004.	Sightseeing Through Whisky Pauvre John ou les Aventures d'un buveur de whisky **Survives**
912–924.	Under the Seas Deux Cents Milles sous les mers ou le Cauchemar du pêcheur also known as Deux cent mille lieues sous les mers **Fragment**	1005–1009.	Good Glue Sticks La Colle universelle **Survives**
		1010–1013.	Satan in Prison Satan en prison **Survives**
		1014–1017.	Delirium in a Studio Ali Barbouyou et Ali Bouf à l'huile **Survives**
925–928.	The Skipping Cheeses Les Fromages automobiles **Survives**	1018–1022.	Bakers in Trouble La Boulangerie modèle **Lost**
929–935.	How Bridget's Lover Escaped Le Mariage de Victorine also known as Le Mariage de Victoire **Survives**	1023–1029.	An Angelic Servant (US) Jewel of a Servant (UK) La Perle des servantes **Lost**
936–950.	Tunneling the English Channel Le Tunnel sous la Manche ou le Cauchemar anglo-français also known as Le Tunnel sous la Manche ou le Cauchemar franco-anglais" **Survives**	1030–1034.	The Knight of Black Art Le Tambourin fantastique **Survives**
		1035–1039.	In the Bogie Man's Cave La Cuisine de l'ogre **Survives**
951–955.	A New Death Penalty La Nouvelle Peine de mort **Lost**	1040–1043.	The King and the Jester François Ier et Triboulet **Survives**
956–960.	Drink! A Great Temperance Story Le Delirium tremens ou la Fin d'un alcoolique **Lost**	1044–1049.	The Good Luck of a "Souse" Il y a un dieu pour les ivrognes **Fragment**

1908

1050–1065. *Humanity Through Ages* also known as *Humanity Through the Ages*
La Civilization à travers les âges **Lost**

1066–1068. *Justinian's Human Torches* also known as *Justinian's Human Torches 548 A.D.*
Torches humaines **Survives**

1069–1072. *The Genii of Fire*
Le Génie du feu **Survives**

1073–1080. *Why That Actor Was Late*
No French release **Survives**

1081–1085. *The Dream of an Opium Fiend*
Le Rêve d'un fumeur d'opium **Survives**

1086–1090. *A Night With Masqueraders in Paris*
Nuit de carnaval **Lost**

1091–1095. *Long Distance Wireless Photography* (US)
Electrical Photographer (UK)
La Photographie électrique à distance **Survives**

1096–1101. *The Prophetess of Thebes*
La Prophétesse de Thèbes **Survives**

1102–1103. *In the Barber Shop*
Salon de coiffure **Survives**

1104–1108. *A Mistaken Identity*
Le Quiproquo advertised with the subtitle *comique* **Lost**

1109–1113. *A Lover's Hazing*
Mariage de raison et Mariage d'amour **Lost**

1116–1123. *A Fake Diamond Swindler*
L'Habit ne fait pas Lemoine ou Fabricant de diamants **Lost**

1124–1131. *Curiosity Punished*
La Curiosité punié ou le Crime de la rue de Cherche-Midi à quatorze heures **Lost**

1132–1145. *No Trifling With Love* also known as *The New Lord of the Village*
Le Nouveau Seigneur du village advertised as a *scène comique à spectacle* **Survives**

1146–1158. *The Miser*
L'Avare **Fragment**

1159–1165. *Sideshow Wrestlers*
Le Conseil du pipelet ou Un tour à la foire advertised with the subtitle *bouffonnerie extravagante* **Survives**

1166–1172. *Pranks With a Fake Python*
Le Serpent de la rue de la Lune **Lost**

1173–1175. *Up-to-Date Clothes Cleaning*
High-Life Taylor (*un complet modern style; originalité*) **Lost**

1176–1185. *The Broken Violin*
Lully ou le Violon brisé advertised with the subtitle *très artistique; spécial pour coloris; anecdote Louis XIV en 4 tableaux, avec ballet* **Fragment**

1186–1189. *Hunting the Teddy Bear*
Tartarin de Tarascon (*une chasse à l'ours comique*) **Lost**

1190. *The Little Peace Maker*
Le Trait d'union advertised as a *gracieuse scène artistique avec apparition* **Lost**

1191–1198. *A Love Tragedy in Spain*
Rivalité d'amour **Lost**

1199–1217. *Mishaps of the New York–Paris Race*
Le Raid New York–Paris en automobile **Lost**

1218–1226. *The Mystery of the Garrison*
Sortie sans permission **Lost**

1227–1232. *The Woes of Roller Skaters* also known as *The Woes of Roller Skates*
No French release **Survives**

1233–1237. *The Magic of Catchy Songs*
No French release **Lost**

1238–1245. *The Forester's Remedy*
No French release **Lost**

1246–1249. *Love and Molasses* also known as *His First Job*
No French release
Known as *Amour et mélasse* **Survives**

1250–1252. *The Mischances of a Photographer*
No French release
Known as *Les Mésadventures d'un photographe* **Survives**

1253–1257.	The Indian Sorcerer Le Fakir de Singapour **Survives**	1367–1371.	Incident from Don Quixote (US) Magic Armour (UK) La Toile d'araignée merveilleuse also known as Aventures de Don Quichotte **Lost**
1258–1265.	Two Crazy Bugs No French release **Lost**		
1266–1268.	A Tricky Painter's Fate (US) A Railway Passenger's Ruse (UK) No French release **Survives**	1372–1385.	No English release La Fée Libellule ou le Lac enchanté **Lost**
1269–1275.	The Hotel Mix-Up also known as At the Hotel Mix-Up No French release **Lost**	1386–1393.	No English release Moitié de polka **Lost**
		1394–1407.	The Fortune Favors the Brave also known as The Genii of the Bells Le Génie des cloches ou le Fils du sonneur **Lost**
1276–1282.	Oriental Black Art No French release **Lost**		
1283–1287.	Two Talented Vagabonds Le Jugement du garde champêtre **Lost**		
1288–1293.	French Interpreter Policeman also known as French Cops Learning English No French release **Survives**	1408–1415.	Hypnotist's Revenge No French release **Lost**
		1416–1428.	No English release Known as Pharmaceutical Hallucinations Hallucinations pharmaceutiques ou le Truc du potard **Survives**
1294–1300.	Fun With the Bridal Party Le Mariage de Thomas Poirot **Lost**		
1301–1309.	Not Guilty Anaïc ou le Balafré **Survives**	1429–1441.	No English release Known as The Good Sheperdess and the Evil Princess La Bonne Bergère et la Mauvaise Princesse **Fragment**
1310–1313.	Buncoed Stage Johnnie Pour l'étoile S.V.P. **Fragment**		
1314–1325.	A Grandmother's Story Conte de la grand-mère et Rêve de l'enfant also known as Au pays des Jouets **Fragment**		
		1442–1459.	The Living Doll La Poupée vivante **Lost**
		1460–1466.	Seein' Things Fin de réveillon **Lost**
1326–1328.	The Helping Hand Pour les p'tiots also known as Le Main secourable **Lost**	1467–1475.	Unknown title(s) **Lost**
		—.	No English release L'Agent gelé **Survives**
1329–1336.	The Old Footlight Favorite Trop vieux! **Lost**	—.	Tribulation or the Misfortunes of a Cobbler No French release **Survives**
1337–1346.	The Wonderful Charm (US) The Marvellous Fountain (UK) La Fontaine merveilleuse **Lost**		
		1909	
1347–1352.	Honeymoon in a Balloon (US) The Ascension of a Communicant (UK) L'Ascension de la rosière also known as Voyage de noces en ballon **Lost**	1476–1485.	The Doctor's Secret Hydrothérapie fantastique also known as Le Secret du Médécin **Survives**
		1486–1494.	Unknown title(s) **Lost**
1353–1366.	A Rude Awakening Pochardiana ou le Rêveur éveillé **Lost**		

1495–1501. The Fiendish Tenant also known as
The Diabolic Tenant
Le Locataire diabolique **Survives**
1502–1507. No English release
Un homme comme il faut **Lost**
1508–1512. No English release
Known as Whimsical Illusions
Les Illusions fantaisistes **Survives**
1513–1521. If I Were King
Si j'étais roi!!! **Lost**
1522–1529. No English release
Le Roi des médiums (apparitions
fantômatiques) **Lost**
1530–1533. The Spider and the Butterfly
Papillon fantastique **Fragment**
1534–1535. No English release
La Gigue merveilleuse **Lost**

1910
No films

1911
1536–1547. No English release
Known as Baron Munchausen's
Dream
Les Hallucinations du baron de
Münchausen also known as Les
Aventures de baron de Munchhausen
Survives
1548–1556. No English release
Known as The Diabolical Church
Window
Le Vitrail diabolique (magie vénitienne)
Fragment

1912
Pathé. No English release
Known as The Conquest of the Pole
À la conquête du Pôle **Survives**
Pathé. No English release
Known as Cinderella or the Glass
Slipper
Cendrillon ou la Pantoufle merveilleuse
Survives
Pathé. No English release
Known as The Knight of the Snow and
The Knight of the Snows
Le Chevalier des Neiges **Survives**
—. No English release
Known as The Voyage of the Bourrichon
Family
Le Voyage de la famille Bourrichon
Survives

INTERVIEWS

Interview with Serge Bromberg

Serge Bromberg is one of those incredible polymaths whose passion for cinema becomes a joyous force within it. He is a film producer and director in his own right, a television presenter, a chairman and director of several film bodies and a champion of the preservation and exhibition of early cinema. For some years, Serge has been forefront in the campaign to find, preserve and screen the missing films of Georges Méliès and in this he has been very successful. He led the team which assembled ultimately 200 films for the definitive DVD Box set 'Georges Méliès – The First Wizard of Cinema' and, in 2011, unveiled an incredible colour restoration of Méliès's most famous film 'A Trip To The Moon'.

Jon Spira: The first thing I'd like to know is really to find out how you would define your place within the Méliès story.

Serge Bromberg: Well, the only person that is central to the Méliès story is Méliès himself. He was instrumental in producing and creating the films, and he's the one who decided in 1923 to destroy all of those negatives and prints. So, at the end of the day, he left us with the heritage, when I mean us [I mean] humanity, with the heritage of trying to locate prints in attics, basements, or, you know, archives, who knows where? Uh, and restore the film. And then share them, and revive the amazement. So the way I see myself in that picture is just being one of those many who have, at some point, saved one of the Méliès films and wanted to share it. But because many archives throughout the world, there are hundreds, have found films over the years, and also because the Méliès family, Madeleine Malthete-Méliès, the granddaughter, and then the great-grandchildren have been scouting around the world to find prints... I mean, all that matters in the end is that we are all film passers. We pass the films on to the next generation. So that's how I see myself. Restoring films is just a technical means to pass the films to the next or the present generations. That's where I'm standing.

JS: That's fantastic. So, for people who may not understand the technical side of things, can you explain why films need to be preserved and restored?

SB: Well, that's very simple. When you have the camera negative of a film, uh, it's a negative. It's like in old photos, maybe those who are only in the digital space will not understand that, but to take a picture in the old days, except for a few systems called reversal daguerreotypes or Polaroid, the system was that you would film onto negative stock, and from that negative stock, you could print as many positive prints as you wanted. The positive prints have many problems. The first problem was unsteadiness, if it was printed wrong. There could be problems of grading, too light or too dark. There could be problems of, uh, decay, once a print starts traveling from one cinema to the other, it can be ruined in the projector, if it's forgotten on the shelf, it can self-destruct by syndromes called decomposition or vinegar syndrome, for the safety film. So there's many, many issues. And worse, if the negative is gone, then that means we do not have the master from which we will be able to print film in the future. So restoring a film is basically taking the best elements that survive that may be endangered because of time, because of the way they were stored in the past, or there can be many reasons. And basically to recreate a new printing master that will be used and will be available to be used in the future to make files, broadcasts, 35 mm prints, I mean, anything. Basically, it's that restoring a film is restoring a new master from which we will be able to disseminate the film throughout the world. So in the case of Méliès, because the negatives were destroyed by Méliès himself, and including [his] prints, the only way we can eventually find the films again, is to locate the print that has been abandoned somewhere, or that ended up in a private collection, I mean, who knows why? He destroyed his films in 1923. In 1929, there was a Méliès, uh, like a tribute evening at the Pleyel... at the Salle Pleyel in Paris. At that moment, only eight films out of the 520 films that he shot did survive, and not all of them complete.

As of today, we have probably about 230 films, which means that in the last let's say 90 years, we have found about 215. So you see, those films could have been found, located, anywhere in the world. Anywhere a film was sent to be presented, 1905, 1910, 1920, and then it stayed there. It never came back. And without the archives, without the collectors, those prints would have been junked. That's our worst competition – the garbageman.

And, uh, so we take those prints that have been... that have circulated, they may be very incomplete, in the case of Méliès, they are of course all silent. They have lines, they have scratches, sprockets are torn, they are shrunken because after some time, the film starts to shrink. They can have local decay, or they can be abridged. All kinds of things. And then, from that scrappy material, or from that scrappy material, and other scrappy prints that have been found around the world, you gather them all, and then you scan them all, and with digital technologies, you reassemble everything, so in the end, you will have a continuous print, or not, of the film.

For example, *Robinson Crusoe* has been restored from the only print that survived, and that print is incomplete. So we have the film, it is stabilized, all the big image problems have been solved digitally. We have made a new score. We have restored the narration based on the catalog description, and so on. But the beginning is missing, the very end is missing, and in the middle, there's a little chunk that is missing. Well, there's nothing else we can do. It's not there to be found, unless sometime, at some point, somebody will find a print somewhere. That I don't know. And the only way to know is to search for the films. But at the end of the day, what we're doing is just trying to get back as close as possible to what Méliès wanted to do, to share it.

JS: So, can you tell me how you personally got involved in this area?

SB: Well, you know, people know me, I'm notorious for being so passionate about these films. I mean, I've been watching films from when I was about ten years old, and at the time... I'm 57. At the time when there were no VCRs, VHS, DVDs and so on, the only thing there was, the only way to watch a film at the time was to buy a Super 8 millimeter or 9.5 print, bring a small projector, put it in front of a screen, close the curtains, and then in the dark, have some kind of messianic (laughs) experience of watching Chaplin on a screen.

And I guess on a... on a ten year old kid, it had... it sometimes can have a minor influence, and on me, it had an influence that is still lasting about 50 years later. And, you know, it is so thrilling, I mean, to find lost treasures, to go back in time, to be basically Dr. Frankenstein. If you remember, Frankenstein is not the monster. Frankenstein is the doctor who can turn back dead bodies into living bodies. Well, basically, I'm turning back dead film cans into laughter and emotion. Can you think of anything more amazing?

JS: That's beautiful.

SB: I can't. *(Laughter)*

JS: Beautiful. So you started as a collector, and...

SB: Yes.

JS: And that's how you edged into this.

SB: Yes. I started as a collector, so, you know, George Bernard Shaw said that the secret of success is to last long enough. So, I started Lobster in 1985 as a production company. But truly, I did not... I mean, I... that was not why I was on Earth. I mean, over the years, I've produced, I've even directed, feature films, but in the end, the reason people know me is for my craziness for classic films and the way I share them with enthusiasm.

JS: And how do you share them? What is your connection to the public?

SB: Oh, all kinds of ways. Lobster is about 25 people working. There's stock shot sales, TV distribution, international Blu-Ray, DVD, screenings, I do concerts where I play piano on silent films, I give courses, I do TV programs, I have a monthly magazine on French television about classic films, and so on. I mean, every way I can share and promote the films, I do. I buy the rights of the films, so I can restore the film, and then finance that restoration by circulating the films. I also spend some, a lot of time, looking for backers and sponsors, because unfortunately, those classic films do not have the let's say financial, uh, resource that most of the time would cover the cost of the restoration, which can be enormous.

So in a way, I'm also a producer of restorations. But you know, who cares [about] the restorer? Uh, I mean, have you read the articles about the restoration of *Trip to the Moon* in color?

JS: Of course, yeah.

SB: Yeah.

JS: And – and I've seen the documentary as well.

SB: Yeah. So that's the plan, you know, when we started in 1999, we were just going nowhere. We were leaving the shore, but not going... not knowing how we would finish that plan, because the technologies that allowed us to finish the restoration were not even conceived when we started digitizing the material. Can you think of anyone crazy enough to spend three years, I mean, scanning frame-by-frame that print that was in shreds, and- and hoping that one day we'd get back… you have to be crazy. I'm proud to be crazy.

JS: *(Laughter)* So Méliès is clearly very important to you personally.

SB: Yeah, Méliès – Méliès is, first of all, Méliès is the symbol of lost films and rediscovered films. Also, Méliès is the DNA of cinema. People always say that Lumiere leads to Rossellini, and Méliès leads to Fellini. And those are the two sides of the brain of the perfect cinema lover. So, yes, I'm amazed in Méliès, but you know, I've also been the director of the Annecy Animation Film Festival for 15 years, so I'm very interested in animation, and I'm fond of slapstick comedies. And I restore French classics that I love, and we do all, you know… I'm a cinevore. I'm just too hungry, and there's not enough film to discover to feed me.

JS: *(Laughter)* So, tell me about your first experience with Méliès. How were you first aware of Méliès?

SB: Well, my first, in Super 8, in the '60s, the film office was distributing in black and white a cut-down version of about six minutes of the *Conquest of the North Pole*…

JS: Mmm.

SB: Which is a 1912 film, which is very bizarre, because Méliès kind of went bankrupt in 1910. 1911, he hardly shot anything, and then he went to Pathé, and told Charles Pathé that he needed money, to make films that would amaze the world. And Pathé did not believe it. So he said to Méliès, "Okay, that's fine, but I want your house as a collateral. So if I lose my money, I'll get the house." And Méliès said yes. He made four films, uh, that were all flops.

JS: Yeah.

SB: So at the end of the day, that's the reason he lost his house, and had to burn his films in 1923. But among those films was that *Conquest of the North Pole*, that ends with the creature supposed to be the yeti, you know, like the man of the North Pole, that is like a huge statue animated with ropes and things like that. And when you watched it, and you can watch it on YouTube, it's so bizarre, (laughter) and that, I watched that, I wondered, why would anyone – anyone do such a thing? And, uh, and that – that was my first meeting with Méliès.

JS: So how old… how old were you then?

SB: Probably ten.

JS: Wow.

SB: I remember it was not even a super 8, it was an 8 millimeter, which was an older gauge at the time.

JS: And that led you on this quest?

SB: Yeah, well, you know. Méliès made about 520 films, and I told you between 220 and 230 do survive, because some of them survive only partially, some of them survive in black and white, whereas they had colours at some point. Some of them survive in only awful prints, full of splices and things that cannot be repaired. So for those, they are still to be rediscovered.

JS: So how many of his films have you been involved with the restorations of?

SB: Well, that's very simple. In 2009, we produced a DVD set with Blackhawk Films and Flicker Alley, called *Méliès: The First Wizard of Cinema*. And the idea at the time was to gather all the Méliès films that were available. Uh, we could, at the time, find 200 films, exactly. So, there was quite a lot. That's more than 90%, 95%, of what existed at the time. So in the next ten years, a lot have been found. Like *Robinson Crusoe*, for example, has been found recently. It was not available at the time. And only a fragment was available at the time. About one minute, and only black and white. And it was found in Holland.

So, you know, maybe we've… we're involved with the restoration of more than a hundred of them, but in the dissemination and presentation and distribution of them, I would say every single piece of Méliès film has gone through us one way or another.

JS: And how does that make you feel?

SB: Um, happy? Some people… some people would say proud.

JS: Yeah.

SB: But, no, I'm not proud. My – my name is not meant to remain on the picture. Only Méliès counts. Not me. So, you know, and it makes… it makes me feel immensely happy, when a young kid watches a Méliès film and without my, and anyone at Lobster, being here, he would not have been able to. But he doesn't even know me. And I'm… that's fine.

JS: What, out of all of the restorations, what was the most complicated, what would you say is your greatest achievement?

SB: Oh, the *Trip to the Moon* without a doubt. I mean, you've seen the documentary?

JS: Yeah.

SB: In that [DVD] set, in the set you have, there's one that is absolutely bizarre, and – and thrilling. But it's very hard to explain, so I will not. But the film called the *Merry Frolics of Satan*; it was restored from seven different elements. Some of them black and white, some of them colour. We tried to remain in the colour space as much as we could, but the colour element, which are only from Europe, no American element, was ever hand-coloured, uh, were not complete. So we completed with an American source, actually the Library of Congress material. And so, it's like a jigsaw puzzle. You see the film switch from one colour space to another, from one very sharp element to a much less sharp element, that at the end of the day, the film is complete and you get the whole idea. And about 80% is in colour. So that's one of the tricky ones but, you know, films like the *Magic Cauldron* and things like that, we have a complete, the only actually surviving complete hand-coloured print on nitrate, made in 1903. And that, we just made a scan, and gave it digital restoration. It was not that complex. You know? But, yeah, I mean, *Trip to the Moon* is certainly one of the very complex ones. The one also that took forever, let's say started at some point and ended at some other, uh, other, it's a film called *Kiriki*.

JS: Tell me about *Kiriki*.

SB: It's a film for which I bought a… I didn't know what it was, it was a Pathé 1907 print, and I bought a 16 mil print from a collector, dealer, in Argentina. We're probably 1986 or 1987. And the print arrived but was black and white, and apparently it was made, I mean, the source was a hand-coloured print, or stencil-coloured, but the print I had was certainly in black and white. So I called the guy and said, "do you have the original material that made that 16 millimeter black and white negative?" And he said "No, I junked it…"

JS: Oh…

SB: "…after making the duped negative." So that was very sad. In 1993, we bought the, let's say we made a deal with the collector, and had access to his entire collection. And in his collection was a print of *Kiriki* that was original vintage nitrate stencil coloured. The only problem is that the film is about 130 meters, which is about 400 feet. And what we had in our hand was just six feet. So it was slightly incomplete, to say the least. It was a very short fragment. But at the same time, we had the colour for each of the characters that were on the picture. So we knew that if one day, we would find a good element, we would be able to reassign the colour to each character, the way they were in 1907. And the miracle happened in the year 2000, where I was at the Cinematheque Francaise with a curator called Claudine Kauffmann, and we were going through the vault, and I see *Kiriki* [written] on a can, and said, "What is it?" Well, it seems to be the camera negative.

JS: Oh… *(Laughter)*

SB: So it had a very special system of one perf, so it could not be printed on standard printers, which is why the Cinematheque Francaise never used it. But at the same time, it was here! So what we did is we made a 35 mil positive print of the camera negative, then we asked my sister, who was a student at the Art Deco School in Paris, to take a brush in the style of the old days and hand-paint every single frame on the new print, with brushes and the chemical colours of the old days. It took also forever, in the year 2000, we could at last deliver the *Kiriki* in colour with the best sharpness one could think of. And of course we published it on DVD, so it was copied and put on YouTube and so on, so you can watch *Kiriki* on YouTube with colours. And of course, no one knows that this is not a vintage colour, because a vintage coloured print does not exist. It's our restoration. But of course, they removed the head title saying this is a restoration from Lobster Films.

JS: Right.

SB: And the Cinematheque Francaise, and Helene Bromberg hand-colored it in the year 2000. And I would like to pay an homage, because she passed away a few years later and she has been so wonderful, and to see her name removed from the history of cinema when she was so great for such a great film, I think it's not… it's not fair.

JS: That's terrible. You want these films to be shared, but you also want… people need to understand the work that has gone into this.

SB: Yes.

JS: Yeah. So, tell me, what do you think the likelihood is of finding more of the Méliès films?

SB: Well, let's say, my guess is that if, in a century, which is about as long as the print would survive, the life of a print is about that. Uh, if the survival rate is 220 prints, I would be amazed if we could find another 30 titles.

JS: Right.

SB: Which means that at the end of the day, it's quite unlikely we'll find half of the Méliès films. Now, you must understand that the first two years, Méliès made a lot of views of Paris…

JS: Yeah.

SB: Without any special traits, they're all documentary views. And those, maybe we have them, but we don't know they are from the Méliès catalogs.

JS: Right.

SB: There were no credits at the beginning or in the end. And he didn't have the Star Film logo at the time. So it's quite likely some of them are still around, but we will never know. And the most important titles were those that were the most distributed. So the likelihood of the survival of major titles is higher than for the obscure ones. So, we can, let's say, consider that we have most of the major and interesting titles.

JS: And- and I know that- that before you found it, the hand-coloured version of *Trip to the Moon* was your holy grail.

SB: Yes. But we didn't find it, it was found in Barcelona in 1993. They could not restore it, because obviously it was not restorable. And we made an exchange, and got access to that print, and actually got it in 1999. It was, well, you know, it's one of those things, people would say, "what is your holy grail?" Well, the *Four Devils* by Murnau, the long version of *Greed*... or *Hats Off*, Laurel and Hardy, or *Her Friend the Bandit* by Charlie Chaplin. You know, and of course *Trip to the Moon* was one of those titles, legendary titles, that we thought would... we would never see. Actually, I never mentioned it, because I had no clue that the film ever existed in colour. So, you know, when the film arrived in colour, we liked the idea that the film would remain very secret until we would make it public.

JS: So, you did an incredible, beautiful job on that restoration. And that obviously came out to great acclaim. So I'm wondering, in terms of the films of Méliès, what's your holy grail now?

SB: Uh... *(Laughter)* Well, you know, I think I found it, but I'm not sure.

JS: Oh?

SB: So I may not mention it.

JS: Okay. *(Laughter)*

SB: But it's a film... it's a film that we have in bad condition that I love, that is one minute. It's absolutely exquisite. And I think we... I found a better print.

JS: Oh.

SB: And I always thought oh, well, this film is so awful that it's hardly watchable. But I'm close to get it back.

JS: That's very exciting to hear.

SB: *(Laughter)*

JS: So, through all of your work, and all of your research, and the time you spent on Méliès' films, I'm interested in what impression you've built up of him as a man. Like, how would you describe his personality, you know, in both positive and the negative, how do you view him?

SB: Well, I will not comment on that, because of the family, they will not want me to say bad things.

JS: Sure.

SB: And of course, no one needs me to say nice things.

JS: Sure.

SB: So... *(Laughter)* so, uh, at the end of the day, he was a man of sweet and sour. I mean, he's... let's say that he had a Jekyll side, but he also had a Mr. Hyde side. He was certainly very stubborn, very demanding, probably hard to have a relationship with. But maybe that's the condition to be a genius, you know? Tati was not easy to deal with, Welles was not, Chaplin was not. But they were Tati, Welles, and Chaplin. So, as far as we could, as we know of, of Méliès, uh, probably at the end of his life, he was nicer, but to be an explorer of the possibilities of film, you need to be so, so everywhere, you know? Sets, acting, directing, camera, businessman, all the inventions he made, hand-colouring and so on. So, I mean, to do all that at the same time, you must be not only a dreamer, you really must be... you know. Even the fact that probably the reason he made all those trick films, besides the fact that he was a magician, is that the Lumiere brothers, didn't want to sell him a camera.

JS: Yeah.

SB: So, he went to Robert William Paul in England, and asked Paul to design a camera, which Paul did. But the camera was not as sophisticated as the Lumiere material. And because of that lack of sophistication, when he was shooting a bus on the Place de l'Opera in Paris, the camera got stuck. And it took him a few seconds to fix it, and when he resumed filming, in the place of the bus, was, how do say? You know, the Hearse. And so he realized, when he was watching the film, that all of the sudden, the bus, I mean, turned into a Hearse, and then that's what gave him the idea that maybe he could do things that real life cannot do. If maybe he had got a Lumiere camera that worked perfectly, he would never have had the idea of doing magic tricks with cinema. Who knows?

JS: When you're in Paris, do you feel a connection to Méliès there?

SB: Well, you know, it's like when you say, uh, go to America and say Lumiere invented cinema. People will laugh at you. If you go to Paris and say Edison invented Cinema, people will scream at you.

JS: Yeah.

SB: But the truth is that the first film ever shot and recorded in the motion picture copyright registry at the Library of Congress was made in 1893. So that's three years before the first public screening of the Lumiere brothers.

JS: Is that *Louis Le Prince*?

SB: No, no, no, no, no. That's *The Sneeze*.

JS: Oh, *The Sneeze*. Okay, right.

SB: Yeah, no, *Le Prince* is 1890 and nothing was ever copyrighted because nothing ever survived.

JS: Right.

SB: Well, some of it survived, but, uh, at the time, nothing survived. And as we all know, *Le Prince* did not survive to ever file anything to any academy of patent.

JS: No. But do you feel, I mean, what I'm getting at is that you exist in a place where Méliès made films, and films which, often, you find yourself working on. I was wondering if that has any resonance for you.

SB: No, I'm working with the same energy on Charlie Chaplin and Buster Keaton.

JS: Sure.

SB: And they were not born in Paris. So, at the end of the day, my country is cinema. It's not, you know, France or America or Argentina or wherever. I mean, my last... my last show, I call them show, but people say, you should call them concerts, or with classic film, with silent films, was in Helsinki, Finland, and it was a week ago, for the opening of the Kino Regina, which is the new theatre of the archive, which is a stunning building.

JS: Oh, wow.

SB: Amazing. Yeah. So, you know, I'm showing films around the world. I'm lucky enough to speak good English. And even better French. so I can go everywhere, and share my passion. It's really a gift, a blessing.

JS: I've just got a couple more questions.

SB: Okay, go ahead.

JS: The first one is, why is Méliès important?

SB: Why is my wife important? Why is drinking good wine important? Why is discovering other countries important? Méliès is the DNA of cinema. And it's pure imagination. Méliès has a level of poetry that is maximum. For those who know Méliès, no explanation is necessary. And for those who don't know Méliès, no explanation is possible.

JS: Perfect. Do you think there is a future for Méliès?

SB: Oh, well, as long as there will be human intelligence, Méliès will be a hero. Yes. That not only is there a future for Méliès, but my guess is that when most of the major cinematographers, or directors, or authors of cinema today, will be forgotten, Méliès will still be there. Because, you know, think of that image of the moon with the rocket in the eye. No one knows it's Méliès, but everyone knows that image.

JS: Absolutely.

SB: So, you know, that's – that's why Méliès is eternal.

JS: And my final question is, what does Méliès mean to you personally?

JS: For me, Méliès is youth. Eternal youth.

JS: That's perfect, Serge. Thank you so much.

SB: All right, there's something I must add that you haven't asked, but I want to insist on, and there was a part of the plan of doing those colour fairytales, you know, that DVD that we just published. (*Les Contes Merveilleux de Méliès en couleurs*, Lobster Films, 2018).

JS: Yeah, absolutely.

SB: Okay. Our idea, doing this, was how can we promote the films, the Méliès cinema, to the next generation? And it's not, you know, the trick films, the early ones, things disappear and reappear and so on, it's too far away for young kids. They will not understand what they're watching. But the Méliès films, I mean those he made in colour, in the 1900s, in the mid-1900s, were used as a base for narration. We called it in French, le bonniment. Bonniment means basically that there is a man behind the screen saying, "...and here is the astronomers that enter in the atelier, and now here is the president, who will present his plan to go to the moon!" And then you see the image, so it was like a live show. Our intention is to put Méliès in that space of narrative cinema, so the kids, when they are young, they will see an image mostly in colour, they probably will not realize at first that it's artificial hand-colouring. They will see someone narrating. So they will think "oh, well, it's interesting." It's like, you know, those books with the fairytales, the Grimm Brothers fairytales and so on. And so they will just watch this, and if the parents give them that to discover, later, when they grow older, they will have that somewhere in their mind, and in 20 years or 25 years from now, they will be, uh, sensitive to the magic of Méliès. What we would dream is that as, you know, my grandmother used to open a fairytale book and tell me a story, we would hope, and that's why we offered on the Blu-Ray or DVD, a music track only, that some parents will tell to their children, hey, do you want me to tell you a Méliès story? And they will show the film, and they will tell the story themselves, with their own words. And that will be an experience of sharing the magic of Méliès between generations, between parents and young kids. And that's something that's a gift to your children, a gift of cinema. And the gift also that opens the mind to the magic, the DNA of magic of cinema, and the DNA of Méliès.

JS: It's interesting you say that because people today generally don't realize that silent films were never silent.

SB: Absolutely. It's even worse. The word silent cinema appeared in 1927, when they made the *Jazz Singer*. Before that, it was only cinema.

JS: These films were created to be shared in that way, and to be just an element for a wider show of music and Magic Lantern slides and vocal performance.

SB: Absolutely. Absolutely. I mean, you know, the producers of the day didn't have the technical means to reproduce colour, or reproduce sounds. But of course that's something they wanted to do! They all wanted to do that, because they wanted the show to be complete. They wanted the film to be like life. And that was the only way they could achieve it – hand-colour, telling stories, making live music in the audience. But it must have been thrilling at the time.

You know, my feeling is that, when you go see *Gravity*, you see special effects that are so stunning that they really look, like, real. But of course you know they are special effects, so you don't dream. Now, when people went in 1902 to see the *Trip to the Moon*... they didn't know what cinema was about! I mean, you know, cinema was just six years old. And they were just watching these guys in stupid suits, and they didn't have helmets or anything, they just had umbrellas, and the set was like a cardboard painting set. But I'm sure a lot of them were convinced that what they saw was the actual moon.

JS: Yeah.

SB: So you see, the dream does not connect with the technical perfection of the film. The dream is something that relates mostly to poetry and to your ability of dreaming. And I think showing these films and sharing them with the kids opens our ability to dream.

JS: So, in a way, we're saying that Méliès is still important.

SB: Oh, I could... of course. Without a doubt. Without a doubt. ★

Interview with Bryony Dixon

Bryony Dixon is the curator of Silent Cinema at the British Film Institute. Her work spans overseeing the restoration of some hugely significant early films, including in 2012, all nine of Alfred Hitchcock's surviving silent films. She is also a writer and co-director of the annual British Silent Film Festival.

Jon Spira: Can you explain what the BFI's involvement is with silent film in general?

Bryony Dixon: Well, the BFI archive collects all British film, so that includes pretty much everything. We've got a good collection of early film because we started collecting quite early and because people always want to collect early stuff. You know, they want to, sort of, trace the origins of things. So, the collection's quite strong because people started to collect the very early stuff quite early on. And it's kind of an international thing, really, because the trade was very international at that time. Film was bought and sold rather than rented. So, it crossed borders and was repurposed and reused, sent really all over the world. So, it's kind of different from film a bit later on.

JS: And what kind of elements do you hold? Like, what physically is in the archive from that period?

BD: It varies a lot, so, I mean, a lot of film from the very early period of course, is quite fragmentary. Because film, you know, is fragile, decays. And also a lot of it's been heavily used for projecting in parts. So, typically films from this era lose their heads and tails, so you're quite often missing bits. And then there's deterioration that can happen. They're often made of nitrate film stock so they decompose. We get a lot of surface damage, we get dirt, scratches and stuff.

So, you'll typically get, you know, a very early film from like the 1890s, will be about 40 feet, 75 feet typically. So it's about a minute of running time, half a minute to a minute, something in that region. They do get longer, so, by the 1900s they're getting into, you know, 100 feet, 150 feet, and upwards from then on. And really into the teens that's when you get the first long films, really long films, over 40 minutes which is what we call a feature.

JS: And what's involved in, in preserving those films?

BD: Again, it depends what you start off with, you know, if you've got a pretty nice, in good order, early generation piece of material, whether that's a print or a negative or something, you can get a very good result from either duplicating it onto modern film stock or by digitally transferring it. There are two routes really, we still do both, so there's still a photochemical route, whereby we might duplicate something on film stock. And increasingly, we digitize material. And then preserve it in that digital format. As well as then keeping the original film. So the original film then goes back into our master film store, which is basically a big fridge. We keep it at about minus four degrees. And quite dry. And that means that the film will stop decomposing and, you know, we can keep in, sort of, stasis for quite a long period of time.

JS: And are you still finding early films at this point?

BD: Mm-hmm. Yep, the occasional piece of early film still comes in. It is getting rare now, but the other thing is we're finding a lot of films that we're looking for in other archives. Because inevitably, you know, archives catalog their material or store it very, very slowly because it's very expensive and time consuming and challenging. I'm working on this thing about early film, Victorian film, and I'm discovering quite a lot of British titles which are out in other collections. And that could be, you know, film archives or it can be private collections, that kind of thing.

JS: Right. So it's out there, it's just not necessarily knowing where it is?

BD: Exactly, and, and this is a good case in point with Méliès for example, because, you know, there were so many known Méliès films, when Serge Bromberg decided to do his big box set of Méliès films, he did a quite clever thing; which was to nab all of the archivists of the big archives when we were at a film festival event together and say "right, let's just sit down and work this out!" *(Laughing).* Then we did and in about an hour, we had found another 12 Méliès titles.

JS: Wow!

BD: Yeah, I know, so it, it was an extraordinary thing. When you sit down and really compare notes. Because we're all busy people, you know, and everybody's working on their own thing. And, you know, we've all got, sort of, 200 emails at any one time. With people going, "have you got this, have you got that, have you got the other?" So, yeah, that was, that was quite a good moment actually. I remember that.

JS: And what did the BFI actually hold in terms of Méliès at that point?

BD: We've got a bunch of stuff. I mean, I can't tell you chapter and verse, without, sort of, looking it up. But we did have, I think we had the original of, an early version of the partie de cartes, the card game film. Very early.

JS: One of the first, yeah.

BD: Yeah, and all sorts of bits and pieces. And the other thing is, you know, quite often people have versions of the same film, with different material in it.

JS: Yeah.

BD: So you might have a bit where, you know, you've got a longer end bit, or a longer beginning bit, or a bit in the middle. Or you might have a colour version, instead of a black and white version, that sort of thing. The Méliès films are scattered all over the world. Because they were so popular I suppose.

JS: Can you explain how, how the Méliès films came to be in, in Britain. Like, what the distribution route was for that, and how popular he was.

BD: Yeah, as I was saying, in the early days, the way that film worked; there were no cinemas, at that time, so, film shows used to happen in theatres, music halls, fairgrounds, town halls, you know, shops would sort of 'pop up', film shows in shops. And films are bought and sold on the open market, you know, there are catalogs that are produced by the manufacturers that produce them. And if you're an exhibitor and you want to do a fairground bioscope show, you go and buy films from the makers. And then, shortly after that you actually get agents who are carrying stock for all the different film makers. So, there's a guy called Philip Wolff, for example, who holds Lumiere films and Méliès films and R.W. Paul films and G.A. Smith films, and so to all these early film makers, he's acting as an agent. Supplying films to the exhibitors, so the guys who go round with the projector, put the show on in these various venues.

So, Méliès is bought and sold, like any other. But he is, fairly immediately very popular. You know, his films have a very strong, cohesive brand identity. He's got a good visual sense and reasonably high production values and there's something about his films which are quite joyful. I think people like them. They're particularly good for things like fairground shows. Because people are expecting, kind of, magic and illusion and fantasy and that kind of thing. So it fits in with what's already going on in those kind of entertainment venues. So, he was instantly a hit, pretty much all over the world. And very widely copied.

JS: And would you say, is it a case that the films were successful, in terms of sales, or was his name known, would the audience have known who he was, and seen them specifically because it was a new Méliès film?

BD: They did quite often put his name on, yeah. So, yes, I think from the start he was a, sort of, brand. There was either the Star brand or Méliès himself as a name, was a name to be conjured with, sure, yeah. And, as I say, people would go to shows that had his name attached. Because, I mean, very early on, of course, what you did was to go and see the exhibitor, as it were. And it's in about 1898/99 that the change happened when people then go to see a Lumiere film or a Méliès film. Or a program of those films. And that's when their names begin to, you know, be bandied about.

JS: You were saying that his films were widely pirated?

BD: Yeah. Well, somewhere remote, like America, because America's a huge territory and they've got film making equipment over there like everyone else, it was relatively easy for them to literally copy stuff. So, they do, also, you know, there are people who remake films almost exactly. I think in the very early days, this was, sort of, okay. Because, you know, people were going to see the film about the train coming into the station. And that's all they were talking about. So, the filmmakers thought, "oh, I'd better make a train coming into a station film" *(Laughs)*. You know, or "I need to make a scene with a magician doing a trick. Or, you know, babies at tea time squabbling over something". You know, it's amazing how many films in the early days are remakes of other films, and this goes both ways, I mean, Lumiere gets copied obviously, so…

JS: Méliès even copied Lumiere with the, with the card game…

BD: They all copy each other.

JS: Right.

BD: So Méliès copies people, people copy Méliès. And the Lumieres are, sort of, routinely copied because they're first in, and the films are popular. So, they're all doing that, and it then, at the turn of the century, there's a little bit of a change, where people – because they're making some money now – they begin to feel that actually, probably, they take a bit more of a dim view of people literally copying their films.

JS: Yeah.

BD: Photographically, but also just generally plagiarizing. So, sort of, attitudes change, and it's at that point that you'll notice the, the brand marks being introduced into a picture.

JS: Right.

BD: So with Méliès it's what, about 1901/1902, something like that, you suddenly get the star symbol being incorporated into the scenery, and stuff like that. So that he couldn't be pirated.

JS: Can I ask you about the British connection to Méliès, which is that, obviously he, he came over when the Lumieres refused to sell him a camera, he came straight over to, to R.W. Paul, and commissioned him to build his first camera. So, I'm interested to know who Paul was and what their connection was.

BD: Yeah, I think it's a bit more complicated than that. You'd need to go a bit further back…

JS: Okay.

BD: Because Méliès had been to London before, as you probably know.

JS: Yeah.

BD: He came to London in 1888, or something, and got to know Nevil Maskelyne at the Egyptian Hall. Which is this magic theatre, famous magic theatre, and that's where he gets bitten by the bug, which is why he then buys the Robert-Houdin theatre in Paris. So he's mates with Nevil Maskelyne, and Nevil Maskelyne works with a guy called David Devant, who's a illusionist. And who, like Méliès, very early on decides that moving pictures is the next best thing. And they both try to get cameras. You can't buy a cinematograph in, in the year 1896, because the Lumieres won't sell equipment. So they go to R.W. Paul. And it looks as if Méliès actually bought his camera from David Devant, rather than directly from Paul.

JS: Oh, I didn't know that.

BD: Yeah, well, that's what he says. It depends whose memoir you believe really.

JS: This is what Devant says?

BD: I don't know of any recorded occasion where R.W. Paul and Méliès meet. David Devant actually says it in his memoirs, that he sold a camera to Méliès. So he presumably was, not only buying equipment from R.W. Paul, but he was also, he might have bought five cameras, and then sold one or two on. So, kind of an agent or something. And it's all about that connection between the magic theaters and the magicians and the, the early film shows.

JS: And who was R.W. Paul?

BD: He's a film maker, he's, you know, our great pioneer. He was an engineer, an electrical engineer, and he was very young actually. He was like 22 or something like that when he got started. And he was making a pirated kinetoscope machine. So he copied the Edison single viewer box. And he commissioned films from Birt Acres, and they then adapted the film for a projector. So that they could project it on a big screen.

JS: Right.

BD: He happens almost simultaneously with the Lumiere Brothers, they're both working on it at the same time. They're first into the field, as it were, with their projected show in London. They actually do their shows on exactly the same day. Um, the train shows. And R.W. Paul has a show at the Alhambra. The Lumieres are at the The Empire, Leicester Square. So they're on at literally next door theatres. So, he's the, the great pioneer, but he's basically a producer rather than a film maker. He, generally speaking, commissions other people to make the films. He also makes a studio quite early on.

JS: So, did Paul not direct any of those films himself?

BD: Depends what you mean by direct. We don't really know, to be honest. He definitely employed people to make films. Some of them he almost certainly made himself, but in many cases, we don't know. Especially for those earlier ones. We know that they listed all the early, the very early ones. We know that the ones that are shot abroad were by a guy called Henry Short. Walter Booth did most of the trick films.

JS: I've kind of read things suggesting that there was a kind of meeting of minds between Paul and Méliès. And that they were, kind of, doing the same thing to some degree. That they were trying to push something.

BD: He [Paul] begins making trick films in, what, 1900, something like that? The first person to do trick films in Britain is G.A. Smith.

JS: Right.

BD: Very early, those are quite early, sort of 1898 or something like that. Sort of photographing a ghost. Corsican Brothers, things like that, reliant on these, again, stage illusions. Corsican Brothers is a thing about twins and the theatrical version relies on a trapdoor, which is called the Corsican trap so you can have a ghost rising out of the ground.

JS: Right.

BD: And then so he employs by photographing a ghost, a superimposition, kind of, shot. You know, double exposures. So those are quite early. And those are pre-Méliès trick films. So, they're all doing the same thing about the same time. But, you know, and it's all about staged trickery.

JS: And so, you would say that Méliès got an amount of inspiration from his trip to London, and that he was around these people who were also developing the same kind of things.

BD: Yeah, he must have come to London about that time, um, in order to buy the camera. Whether it was off David Devant, or Paul himself. And, you know, it's likely that he was concerned with the nascent film industry. He could have gone to see stuff. But that would have been in 1896. So, whether he then went back in the meantime, nobody knows, I don't suppose. He may have seen some of their stuff in France, or he may not. It's perfectly possible they all had the same idea at the same time, without being influenced by each other.

JS: Yeah.

BD: It's perfectly possible. So, you know, it's quite difficult to say, so and so did it, and so and so, and so and so...

198

JS: Because they were all doing basically the same thing at exactly the same time.

BD: Well, you know, it's in the ether, and so many of them, so many of the guys making the films were stage illusionists. So, you've got Walter Booth, you've got Méliès, you've got Felicien Trewey, who's an illusionist, who then works for the Lumiere Brothers. You know, there's quite a few of them. Nevil Maskelyne, of course, David Devant makes some films, actually he made them with R.W. Paul. So, presumably Paul is behind the camera, or he's with somebody behind the camera. But, you know, so it's all, quite difficult to unpick. Because we don't have good reliable date sources for a lot of this stuff. Some of it's unknowable.

JS: So, what is Méliès' legacy within British cinema?

BD: I think the key thing about Méliès is that sort of fantasy thing, obviously. So it's a filmic version of all that. It's a Victorian theatre, kind of, fantasy. And it's the suspension of disbelief, that a film maker can make. What great personality and some skill, can bring, I think, is his big influence. He makes the film industry better, because his films are beautiful. It sounds a bit simplistic, but, he raises the bar quite high. His personality comes out in his films I think. They've got a sense of humour. He strives for the highest possible production values, they're not cheap, they're, sort of, aspirational in that people go and see Méliès films, people who can't afford to go to the Cirque d'Hiver, or whatever, in Paris and see one of those big spectacular fairy plays or pantomime things. They are very good. Even, even now, people like them instinctively. They're witty.

JS: They're almost the first instance of film being used as art as well.

BD: Art?

JS: Yeah.

BD: In what respect?

JS: As in, it's a work of artistry, what he's doing. Although it's, kind of, wrapped up in commercialism. One of the reasons that his work still endures is because it's artistically sound. It's not just a gimmick, like so much of the stuff that surrounded it was.

BD: Yeah, I mean, I'm slightly cautious about using the word, art, because, you know, if he believed that that was the case, then fair enough. It's quite difficult to label them in that way. He was more of a very, very good story teller. And a visual story teller.

JS: He definitely refers to himself as an artist.

BD: You know, it, it's such a loaded word. I'll leave you to struggle with that one. *(Laughing)* ★

Interview with Michel Gondry

Michel Gondry is one of the most respected modern French filmmakers. Cutting his teeth in the highly creative world of music video, he went on to take his brand of surreal science fiction, fantasy and comedy to Hollywood with his debut feature film 'Eternal Sunshine of the Spotless Mind'. He is renowned for his innovative use of practical effects and in-camera optical tricks over the use of digital techniques. This is a partial transcript of an interview I conducted with him in 2014 for the British Film Institute and is reproduced with their kind permission. It's brief but demonstrates the enduring influence Méliès has to this day.

Jon Spira: What's your earliest memory of science fiction?

Michel Gondry: I remember watching *2001 A Space Odyssey*, not when it first came out, it was in the late seventies. But this scene had a specific impact on me – when they go out in space and start to [experience] a lack of oxygen. I couldn't breathe anymore. I was going to die and I had to leave the screen, the theatre for a few minutes and come back because I couldn't breathe. This movie had a huge impact on me. It's still one of the most expansive films to ever be done. I think it's great. It hasn't aged. And it's a non-return journey.

One time, I [had] a dream and then I made this dream as a short film. I was visiting my childhood house and I was underwater. And then I saw myself in the mirror in the bathroom and I was very old in the reflection. Right about to die. And then I made a short film of it, which was on my first DVD. And when I watched it, I realised that's a rip-off of 2001. And then I said "I dreamt it, I transformed it, and then it belongs to me now".

JS: Has it influenced your work?

MG: I'm not sure it's had any influence on my work. As a director, I'm very careful not to be influenced by directors like Stanley Kubrick, even Orson Welles – directors that went at the end of visual presentation. They are like the end of an evolutionary branch and you can't go anywhere from there. It's like Martin Scorsese, they pushed it so far that if you take from them, it's going to be a replica. And for me, it's very important – maybe I believe I'm their equal, which I know is not true – but it's like *Apocalypse Now*, any movie that will take on this work will be derivative of it. I don't want to be derivative.

JS: Does Science fiction influence your work at all?

MG: Well, in a way, because the initiator of science fiction is Georges Méliès, who was the first one who took the camera, which was just invented, and used it to create a world that was not earthly. I mean, he put people on the moon and he made magical tricks, teleportation, all this sort of stuff. And I think every director of science-fiction refers to him. So, I think that's where it started. Filmmaking divided there between what the Freres Lumieres were doing – which is 'shoot the life' – and what Méliès was doing which was 'invent the life'. Invent a new way of life.

JS: People often draw parallels between you and Méliès.

MG: Yeah, I guess it's very flattering and I try to use imaginative ways to represent what is going on in my head.

JS: Obviously he didn't have a choice, but you use physical effects to a large degree. Can you tell me about that choice?

MG: It's not a choice I do all time, because I did videos for The Chemical Brothers and others that were finished with a computer and it's pretty complicated and I did one for The Rolling Stones where it was only digital effects, so I'm not not, like, stuck in the past, but I think for certain effects, like transitions or dreamy states, like I did for *Eternal Sunshine* or *The Science of Sleep* or *Mood Indigo*, I think that digital technology is used a lot of times to mimic what was done before. On film or in practical effects. So when I want to do an effect which reflects that, I resort to it physically. It's harder, but it involves more the actor in the world. They can perceive the world, or the magic, or whatever's going on around them when they act. So it reflects on their connection between the world and themselves and they feel something else is going on.

JS: It's more organic?

MG: Yeah, it's more organic, yes.

JS: As a genre, why do you think science-fiction is important?

MG: Well, it's sort of... everybody thinks of the future. It's a vision of the future. At times, it shapes, as well, the future. Like *Blade Runner*, I know when Ridley Scott was looking for the look of his characters, thought to take something back, like the punk look, but he thought in the future kids would come back to this punk look at times – it's a cycle. And, I think, in a way he perceived it and in a way influenced it. Because, maybe at some point a kid of a new generation would watch *Blade Runner* and want to dress like *Blade Runner*. So [science-fiction] is a way to feel the future and shape it at the same time, which is quite amazing.

JS: And what is your personal attachment to science fiction?

MG: Well, it just takes me away. It's seeing the future and commenting on the present, and I think that's very important. ★

THANKS

THE FIRST AND BIGGEST THANK YOU MUST GO TO ALL OF THIS PROJECT'S KICKSTARTER BACKERS FOR THEIR KIND SUPPORT AND ENTHUSIASM:

Adam Shepherd	Bob Friedstand	Dan Atwell	Dennis Doros
Adrian Ashton	Brendan Cornwell	Dan Auty	Derek Vickers
Agusti Filomeno	Bret Burks	Dan Judge	Don E Ward
Alan Howard	Brian Anthony	Dan Leonard	Donna Beaney
Alan J Abrams	Brian Lyons	Dan Whitehead	Dora Bertram
Alex Barrett	Brian Macken	Daniel Paxton-Boyd	Dorothée Bertrand
Alex Krebs	Brian Ratigan	Daniel Trembirth	Doug Leedham
Amirf	Britta Carlson	Danny Kelly	Doug Murray
Anders	Brownbagcomics	Darrell Hannan	Dustin Bragga
Andrew and Bethany Payne	Bryan Marshall	Darrell Maclaine-Jones	Emily Wilson
Andrew Daley	Carly	Darren Németh	Emma Pear
Andrew David Barker	Caroline Summers	Darren Reid Cov-Uni	Eric Serna
Andrew Duncombe	Catheryne Hill	Darren Savage	Erica
Andrew Sherburne	Chris Barwick	Darwin Franks	Erika Larsen
Andrew Wille	Chris Grosvenor	Dave	Ethan Beck
Andy	Chris Wysard	Dave Gilyeat	Ethan Gordon
Andy Haigh	Christian Bell	Dave Motion	Evan Dec
Andy The Sane	Christian Koenig	David Babsky	Fallen Dominion Studios
Angela Elvin	Christina David	David Bailey	Fareez Suleiman
Angela Gunn	Christopher "Kier" Conroy	David Kolenda	Fotios Zemenides
Anthony Lawrie	Christopher Davis	David L. Gill	Fred W Johnson
Astrid Goldsmith	Christopher Staples	DAVID MACLEOD	Freja B. Nielsen
Barbara N. Brown	Christopher Tang	David Martineau	Fru Jeune
Baron Carlito	Chuck Ivy	David Morgan	Galen Wilkes
Bartosz Panek	Cindy Womack	David Nolan	Garrett Coakley
Ben Freeman	Clive Shaw	David Quick	Garry Porter
Ben Nicholson	Conrad Hughes	David W. Sanderson	George Guzman
Ben Rive	Craig Barron	David Whittam	Gill Walker
Beverly Hayashi	D.	Deborah White	Gillian Vernon
Bill	D'Arcy Boehm	Debbie Young-Somers	Ginger Stampley
Bill Redmann	Daniel S Turner	Denise Reinert	GingerSnapps

Giovanni Paladini
Havva
Helen Langdon
Henry Fosdike
Henry Meredith
Howard Kistler
Hunt Emerson
Ian Cadwallader
Ian Ericson
Ian Gair
Ian Mantgani
Ian McDonald
Iraj Vaezzadeh
Irene
Isaiah Whisner
Jaakko Kemppainen
Jack Piephoff
Jackie Grieff
Jackie McClements
Jacob Jackson
Jacob Wendt Jensen
Jaik S.
Jaimes Dott
Jake Wilson
Jakub Demianczuk
James Chanter
James Dangerfield
James Pirie
James Schloegel
James Story
Jamie Graham
Jana Johnson
Jane Giles
Jane Harris
Janine Gove
Jasper Sharp
Jaq Greenspon
Jay Spence
Jeff Huisman
Jeff Shaw
Jennifer Kirstein
Jens
Jeremy Burbick
Jerolyn Crute Sackman
Jesse Ephraim
Jessica
Jesterbomb
JF F
JFL
Jim Heine
Jims
Joe Bausch
Joe Kinrade
John Lovick
John McDonald
John Pilbeam
JohnVV
Jon Davison
Jonathan Garvey
Jonathan Wakeham
Jordan Moshe
Jorge Mendonca
Joseph D. Moore
Josh
Josh Wucher
Joy Chao
Juan Gil Rodriguez
Juan Soto
Justin White
Justin Yost
Kamiel De Bruyne
Karim Theilgaard
Kashif
Kate Stock
Kate Youd
Katherine
Kathryn S. Kraus
Katie Pridige
Ken Viola
Kenneth Van Aken
Kerry McKenna
Kevin Eastwood
Kevin John Charbeneau
Kevin Lyons
Kevin Mayle
Kiera Exley
Kim Searcy
Kim Aubry
Kirsty Durham
Kjetil Schjander Luhr
Kristian Martin
Kristofer Olson
Krystel Brown
Ksenia Firsova
Kurt Nettleton
Laura Adams
Laura Cornelius
Laura Marie Scott
Laurent Mertens
Laurie Edwards
Lee Currid
Lee Philipson
Leon Xavier Finch
leonard eshuis
Lisa Jones
Liz
Lonnie Butherus
Luis
Luis Balbosa
M Chew
Mahdi Gilbert
Mara Gibson
Marc Ronnie
Marc Rouleau
Marcia Hines
Mark Boszko
Mark Fuller
Mark Rance
Mark S Zimmer
Mark Turner
Martín Arias
Martin Mulcahy
Martin Shann
Mary Angela Rowe
Mat Froggatt
Mathew Lyons
Matthew Lister
Matthew Searle
Mauricio Reyes
Megan Felicity James
Megan Graieg
Mel
Mendou
Merav Hoffman
Michael Tallon
Michael Walker
Mike Bent
Mike Cassella
Mike Cook
Mike Moran
Mike Shema
Mitch Thompson
Natasha Chisdes
Nathan Wilson
Neil Kenny
Niall McMahon
Nicholas Folsom
Nick Portsmouth
Nico Nimz
Nigel Summerton
Niko Ranta
Nobiloo
Olivia Marsh
Olivia Rohan
Pamela Butler
Pamela Hutchinson
Paul
Paul Lafferty
Paul Male
Paul Sanders
Paul Trinies
Paul Worts
Peter Allen
Peter Cassidy
Peter Hearn
Peter Sloan
Peter Webber
Peter Young
Phil Campbell
Ralf Steinberg
Randall Cyrenne
Randall D. Larson
Rasti Chynoransky
Raúl
Rebecca Blackmore
Rena Kiehn
Rex Baylon
Rhel
Rich Ragsdale
Richard J D A Gorick

Richard Miller	Sara Marsden	Stephen Taylor	Tom
Kirsty Durham	Sasha Hornby	Steve Joyce	Tom Knott
Robbie Wilson	Scott	Steve Messam	Tom Sharp
Robert Deveau	Scott Barden	Steve Wells	Tony Hardy
Robert Hornak	Scott Hughes	Steven Hall	Torkjell Stromme
Robert T. Garcia	Scott McKinnon	Steven Higgins	Trond Hugo Ahlsen
Ronan Kelly	Sean Clouden	Steven Smith	Véronique Gilson
Ross Early	Sean Marsh	Stuart Alexander Arnott	Victoria
Ross Lawhead	Sean Grassia	Stuart Hadley	Vincent Laine
Roy Ferré	Shade Rupe	Stuart Witts	Warren F. Cox
Rudi Endresen	Shane Doyle	Susan Young	Widgett Walls
Russ Williams	Shannon Gordes	Tara Megan	William Barclay
Russell J. Hall	Shaun Buswell	Terry Baxter	William Charles Morrow
Sabina Yun Tang	Sherylee Anne Houssein	Thijs Van Quickenborne	William Davis
Sam Ashcroft	Siddharath Saigal	Thomas Bourke	William Mawdsley
Sam Johnson	Simo Muinonen	Thomas Bull	William Pace
Sam Kimelman	Simon Bleasdale	Tieg Zaharia	Zac Pelkowski
Samuel Hutchinson	Simon Lord	Tiki Murray	Zach Heider
Sand & Wesley	Simon Thomason	Tim Tucker	Zachary Spears
Sandro	Stephen Bissette	Timothy Lambert	Zanniew
Sandy Eisen	Stephen Bruce	Tina Woelke	Zeilenrausch
Sara Cannon	Stephen Gallagher	Todd A. Schall-Vess	

THIS PROJECT WOULD NOT HAVE BEEN POSSIBLE WITHOUT THE SUPPORT AND HARD WORK OF THE FOLLOWING PEOPLE. MY DEEP PERSONAL GRATITUDE GOES TO:

My wife Jen for her endless patience and support.

Jojo and Max Windich for advice, enthusiasm and wisdom.

Ian Nixon, who was a pleasure to work with and produced a beautiful, meticulous translation of a text which was as complicated, enigmatic and whimsical as the man who wrote it.

Lucy Collin for being a wonderful illustrator and a patient old friend.

Simon Minter for his fantastic design work and immaculate pagination.

Nolen Strals for producing the exquisite shiny cover art of this book.

Anne-Marie Malthête-Quévrain, the great-granddaughter of Georges Méliès for long emails full of fantastic information.

Serge Bromberg and Bryony Dixon for their time, insight and enthusiasm.

Graham Humphrey and Nick Rhodes for the stunning art they produced to accompany this project.

Laura Spira for proofreading and tense-watch.

And also...

Brian Sturgulewski at Flicker Alley

Antoine Angé at Lobster Films

Raphael Millet

Corinne Mateo

Susie Dent

Dr Darren Reid

Henry Barnes

Kerry Meacham and Steve Perdue

Dave Gilyeat

The Spira Family

Select Bibliography

Encyclopedia of Early Cinema edited by Richard Abel (Routledge, 2004)

Marvellous Méliès by Paul Hammond (Gordon Frazer, 1974)

Georges Méliès: The Birth of the Auteur by Elizabeth Ezra (Manchester University Press, 2000)

Georges Méliès: Father of Film Fantasy by David Robinson (BFI Publishing, 1993)

Georges Méliès Mage et Mes Memoires by Maurice Bessy & Lo Duca (Prisma Editions, 1945)

A Trip to the Moon Back in Color by Various (Groupa Gan Foundation For Cinema/Technicolor Foundation For Cinema Heritage, 2011)

Who's Who of Victorian Cinema edited by Stephen Herbert and Luke McKernan (BFI Publishing, 1996)

Studios before the system: Architecture, Technology and the emergence of Cinematic Space by Brian R. Jacobson (Columbia University Press, 2015)

Letters by Auguste and Louis Lumiere (Faber and Faber, 1995)

A Chronology of the Cinema Volume 1 from the Pioneers to 1960 by Mirko Riazzoli (Riazzoli, 2017)

A Second Life: German Cinema's First Decades edited by Thomas Elsaesser and Michael Wedel (Amsterdam University Press, 2014)

Fantasia of colour in Early Cinema by Tom Gunning, Joshua Yumibe, Giovanna Fossati and Jonathon Rosen (Amsterdam University Press, 2015)

Forever Ealing: A Celebration of the Great British Film Studio by George Perry (Pavilion Press, London, 1981)

World Film Directors Volume One: 1890-1945 by John Wakeman (The H.W. Wilson Company, 1987)

From Caligari to California: Erich Pommer's Life in the International Film Wars by Ursula Hardt (Berghahn Books, 1996)

Texas Hollywood by Frank Thompson (Maverick Publishing Company, 2002)

Hollywood and the Law edited by Paul McDonald, Emily Carman, Eric Hoyt, Philip Drake (BFI Publishing, 2015)

The Third Eye: Race, Cinema and Ethnographic Spectacle by Fatimah Tobing Rony (Duke University Press, 1996)

The Silent Cinema Reader edited by Lee Grieveson & Peter Kramer (Routledge, 2003)

Pathé: a la Conquete du Cinema 1896-1929 by Stephanie Salmon (Editions Tallandier, 2014)

Nordisk Films Kompagni 1906-1924 Volume 5: The Rise and Fall of the Polar Bear by Isak Thorsen (John Libbey Publishing, 2017)

International Meetings and Congresses of the Film Manufacturers held in Paris, 1908-1909. French Viewpoints by Jean-Jacques Meusy

Silent Cinema: A Guide to Study, Research and Exhibition by Paolo Cherchi Usai (BFI Publishing, 2018)

The Missing Reel by Christopher Rawlence (Harper Collins, 1990)

Eadweard Muybridge: The Human and Animal Locomotion Photographs edited by Hans Christian Adam (Taschen, 2014)

History of Film by David Parkinson (Thames & Hudson, 1995)

Films and DVDs

The Extraordinary Voyage dir. Serge Bromberg and Eric Lange

Gaston Méliès and his Wandering Star Film Company dir. Raphael Millet

The First Film dir. David Wilkinson

Georges Méliès: First Wizard of Cinema (1896-1913), Lobster Films/Flicker Alley

R.W. Paul The Collected Films 1895-1908, BFI DVD

Before the Nickelodeon: The Early Cinema of Edwin S. Porter, BFI DVD

Early Cinema – Primitives and Pioneers, BFI DVD

Lumiere!, France Televisions Distribution/Institut Lumiere

Websites

anthonybalducci.blogspot.com/2014/11/musings-on-andre-deed.html

www.screenonline.org.uk/film/id/514149/index.html

sourcesprotectionsociale.audiens.org/document/la-residence-retraite-du-cinema-et-du-spectacle-35

thebioscope.net/2010/01/12/melies-in-3d ★

About the Authors

Georges Méliès (1861–1938) was one of the most significant and influential pioneers of cinema. Already an illusionist, artist and skilled mechanic, Méliès was the first filmmaker to fully embrace and explore the notion of fantasy in cinema and is credited as the progenitor of sci-fi, fantasy and horror cinema. Creator of many special effects, including multiple exposure and the dissolve, he is regarded still as one of cinema's greatest innovators.

Jon Spira is a writer and documentary filmmaker based in London, England. He has directed two feature films: *Anyone Can Play Guitar* and *Elstree 1976*. Between 2013 and 2016, Jon was the in-house documentary filmmaker and video interviewer for the British Film Institute. His feature documentaries *Anyone Can Play Guitar* and *Elstree 1976* are available on the usual platforms. He has written about film for the BFI, BAFTA, the *Huffington Post* and *The Daily Telegraph*. His previous books are *Videosyncratic: A Book about Life in Video Shops* and *The Forgotten Film Club*. For more info visit **www.jonspira.co.uk** and to stay up-to-date on future projects, follow Jon Spira on Kickstarter.com.